OUR PRESENT EARTH *and the* NEW EARTH TO COME

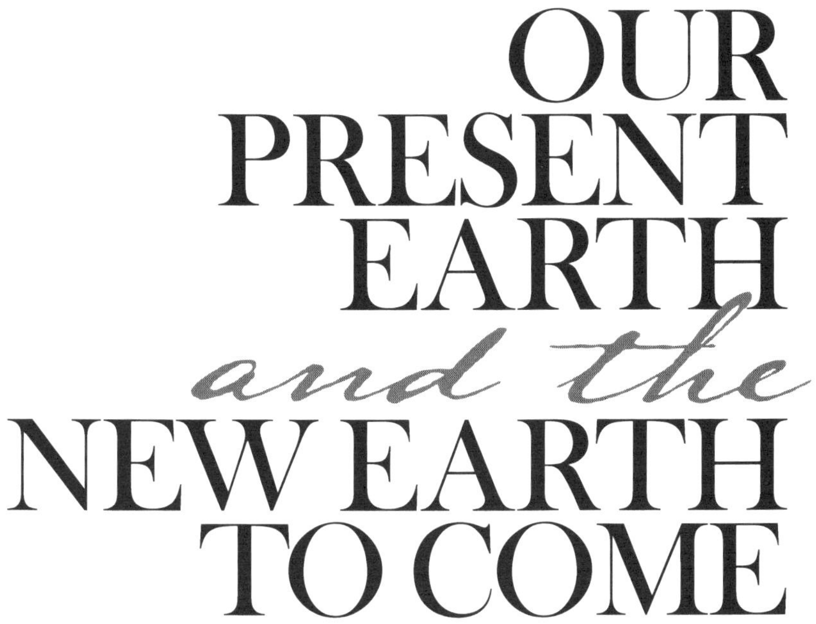

Harley Denny

Scripture taken from the King James Version of the Bible.

ISBN: 978-1-4834-5627-0 (sc)
ISBN: 978-1-4834-5626-3 (e)

Lulu Publishing Services rev. date: 10/10/2016

DEDICATION

I dedicate this book to all my readers who are interested in learning about the future of Our Present Earth that will be replaced by The New Earth created by God for the saved earthly men and women both Jews and Gentiles who managed to live thru the Tribulation Period that accepted God and Jesus as their savior and the Bride of Christ to live on.

CONTENTS

AUTHOR'S INTRODUCTION

My name is Harley Denny and today I present this book as my pulpit to share with my readers my thoughts, understanding and revelation given to me by God thru the Holy Ghost concerning Our Present Earth and The New Earth to Come.

I consider myself a Christian layman, a watchman and servant of my Father God and Savior Jesus Christ my Lord.

My writings and teachings are not influence by any Religionist Denomination or teaching from any Bible Seminary but only thru Gods' revelation given to me by the Holy Ghost during my personal study of His Holy Word.

I have been married to a wonderful lady, Elizabeth Ann, for fifty three years as of December 22, 2015 and I would like to offer my appreciation to her for listening and being so patience with me because she gets to hear all the revelations given to me from God before they are written in my books. We have endeavored to serve God faithfully to the best of our ability while working in several churches filling many capacities during our married life and now a new chapter in our lives has evolved thru the writing of Christian books that I believe are inspired by God thru the Holy Ghost.

We are blessed with wonderful children, Traci and her husband Kevin, Brent and his wife Shannon and four wonderful beautiful granddaughters Jamin, Jacee, Devynn and Zoe and three terrific great grandchildren, Gabriela, Brylee and Elias and a host of wonderful friends.

Ann and I consider ourselves two very happy, grateful proud parents and grandparents.

If you think I sound a little prideful when talking about my family, well I guess you are right. I consider myself a highly favored and blessed man by God.

If you are interested in Bible prophecy and want to know more concerning your future while living on this present earth and in the new earth to come you may want to purchase and read the following book also written by this author.

The Final Destination of Man as described in the Book of Revelation.

Author's e-mail address: hdennybooks@cox.net and you can find me on Facebook under the name of Harley Denny.

FOREWORD

I submit the following about my life, my studies and writings in this book concerning Our Present Earth and The New Earth to Come.

God was and is the spiritual author. I am the earthly co-author chosen by God thru the Holy Ghost to pin down His revelation of His Holy Word for the edification of the readers of this book.

It was during a night in August 2015 that the following words were pressed into my subconscious mind while I was sleeping, Our Present Earth and The New Earth to Come.

I awoke and my immediate thought was, what is God trying to tell me and what am I supposed to do with these words? The Holy Ghost prompted my spiritual man immediately and said write about these words in a new book.

I believe God working thru the Holy Ghost will give us thoughts inserted into our subconscious mind even though we may be totally asleep. We need our spiritual man to be sensitive to Gods' Holy Spirit working thru the Holy Ghost whether we are awake or asleep.

Early the next morning at the beginning of my study and prayer time I said, okay God you have given me a title for a new book by the Holy Ghost that scripture says will teach me all things and now I need you to give me insight into Your Holy Scriptures and embed into my mind the thoughts that You want me to write about concerning this title.

When you read or hear a teaching that is different from what you have been taught and believe, don't just close your mind before you check it out, remember the teaching of Jesus was very different than the teaching of the Scribes and Pharisees during His time on earth. I encourage you to go to your Bible and examine the scriptures for yourself to see what Gods' word actually says. Don't just accept what you hear verbally or what you might read in some book other than the Bible.

I always endeavor to back up my teachings with scriptures found in Gods' Holy Word, if not I will tell you when I give my personal beliefs.

THEMES: MANKIND'S JOURNEY THRU TIME-PAST-PRESENT AND FUTURE

You will realize while reading this book that I have inserted some thoughts and imaginations given to me by God thru the Holy Ghost into stories found in Gods' Holy Bible concerning what men and women may have been experiencing every day as they lived their daily lives on our present earth. These were real people with everyday problems similar to what each of us encounter today.

These are not fiction stories but these are creative non-fiction real life stories concerning men and women that lived good lives along with some who lived bad lives.

The people we read and study about in the Bible did not have the printed words found in our Bible to use as an example to live their lives by as we do today.

Their lives became the printed word that we enjoy reading about today.

We can use their lives as examples as we live our lives during our journey on this present earth. Just be sure to pick out the good lives for your example to live by not the bad ones.

So please read the stories and scriptures that I have provided from Gods' Holy Word and enjoy the stories about the people I selected to write about found in the Bible with an open mind. These were real human beings who lived their lives everyday just like we do on our present earth.

All scriptures used in the writing of this book are from the King James Version of the Bible which I believe was inspired by the Holy Ghost and translated by holy men of God.

MY CHRISTIAN BELIEFS

Romans 1: [16] *For* ***I am not ashamed of the gospel*** *of Christ: for it is the power of God unto salvation to every one that believeth; to the Jew first, and also to the Greek*

I believe the Bible is the inspired word of God.

I believe Gods' message printed in our Bible was and is for all men and women who lived on our present earth past, present and future, and it presents Gods' plan of salvation for all who will accept His Son Jesus as their Savior.

I believe God created the Heaven and the Earth and that Jesus Christ is the Son of God and Jesus was with God when He created the Heaven and Earth.

I believe God sent Jesus to our present earth as a baby born in a manger in a stable in the city of Bethlehem conceived by the Holy Ghost thru a virgin maiden by the name of Mary.

I believe at the age of thirty-three Jesus paid the ultimate price, death by crucifixion on an old rugged cross thus offering himself as a sacrifice for our redemption from sin so we could be reconciled with God.

I believe after three days and nights in the tomb that Jesus rose victorious over sin, death and the grave and He is alive today sitting at Gods' right hand in Gods' Throne Room in Heaven.

I believe thru His death on the cross salvation was offered as a free gift from God for all who will accept His Son Jesus as their Savior and ask for the forgiveness of their sins. It is not something that we can earn by just doing good works although good works is essential in our lives to be a productive Christian.

Galatians 2: [16] *Knowing that a man is not justified by the works of the law, but by the faith of Jesus Christ, even we have believed in Jesus Christ, that we might be justified by the faith of Christ, and not by the works of the law: for by the works of the law shall no flesh be justified.*

I believe Jesus is now seated at the right hand of God making intersession for us as our High Priest but will return to our present earth soon as the KING of KING's and LORD of LORD's at which time He will establish God's earthly Kingdom and rule all nations for one thousand years known as the Millennium reign of Christ.

I believe the men and women who accept Jesus as their Savior while living on our present earth during the One Thousand Year Millennium will be rewarded to live on Gods' New Created Earth described in Revelation Chapter 21 for eternity.

I believe the unsaved men and women who reject Jesus as their Savior will be judged at the Great White Throne Judgment and they will be rewarded by being cast alive into the Lake of Fire to live and suffer for eternity.

I believe in the Trinity Godhead made up of God the Father, God the Son and God the Holy Ghost.

I believe the books of the Old Testament were written primarily for the Jewish people concerning the Nation of Israel to remind them about their past history and the future for the Nation of Israel.

I believe the Old Testament contains prophecies and many scriptures concerning the final end times and the final destination of mankind as recorded in the New Testament.

I believe the prominent figure of the Godhead found in the Old Testament was our LORD GOD Himself.

Many people believe that the messages found in the Old Testament are not for the Church today but I believe we can find a lot of good examples in the Old Testament for us to pattern our lives by while living on this present earth.

I believe the New Testament was written to remind all men, women, boys and girls of the history and future destination of the Church who will become the Bride of Jesus Christ the Son of God. It also describes the final destination for those who reject Jesus as their Savior.

I believe Jesus who is the Son of God is the second entity of the Godhead and the following books Matthew, Mark, Luke, John and the book of Acts Chapter One, Verses One thru Nine describe His life while living on our present earth and His death on the cross.

I believe Jesus died and gave His life as a blood sacrifice so that we might have the opportunity to be reconciled back to God.

I believe Jesus after His ascension back to Heaven sat down at the right hand of God the Father and is now our High Priest making intersession for us. He is our representative and intercessor to Father God as seen in the following scriptures.

Hebrews 4:

[14] *Seeing then that we have a great* ***high priest****, that is passed into the heavens, Jesus the Son of God, let us hold fast our profession.*

[15] *For we have not an* ***high priest*** *which cannot be touched with the feeling of our infirmities; but was in all points tempted like as we are, yet without sin.*

I believe God is a living God and so is Jesus the Son as seen in the following scripture below.

Matthew 16: [16] *And Simon Peter answered and said, Thou art the Christ, the Son of the living God.*

John 6:

[68] *Then Simon Peter answered him, Lord, to whom shall we go? Thou hast the words of eternal life.*

[69] *And we believe and are sure that thou art that Christ,* ***the Son of the living God.***

Hebrews 1: [3] *Who being the brightness of his glory* ***(speaking of Gods Glory),*** *and the express image of his person* ***(Jesus is the image of God),*** *and upholding all things by the word of his* ***(Gods)*** *power, when he* ***(Jesus)*** *had by himself purged our sins, sat down at the right hand of the Majesty* ***(God)*** *on high;*

I believe these verses prove that God and Jesus are both alive and setting on thrones in Gods' Throne Room presently located in Heaven. It says that Jesus sat down on the right hand of the Majesty which is God on high.

I believe the Holy Ghost who is the third entity of the Godhead is the God Person present on the earth we live on today.

I believe that we must still worship God the Father and God the Son Jesus but their Holy Spirits are manifested thru the Holy Ghost to us on our present earth.

John 4: [24] *God is a Spirit: and they that worship him must worship him in* ***spirit and in truth.***

Jesus said after His ascension back to Heaven that He would ask His Father God to send us another comforter which is the Holy Ghost and the term of the Holy Ghost on earth began in the book of Acts, Chapter One Verse Ten and continues to the end of the book of Revelation.

This is found in John 14:16 which state's the Holy Ghost is our comforter.

The physical presence of God and Jesus on earth ended when Jesus ascended back to Heaven to set on His throne at the right hand of God than God sent the Holy Ghost the third entity of the Godhead who is the one present on earth today. The spiritual presence of Father God and Jesus are manifested thru the Holy Ghost to us living on this present earth.

Sometimes we Christians get excited and make statements or show outward emotions in church without thinking about what we are saying or doing. These statements and outward emotions may cause someone in the congregation who is not grounded in Gods' word to get very confused.

Sometimes I get confused when I hear ministers and teachers during their sermons or teachings intertwine God the Father, Jesus the Son, Holy Spirit and the Holy Ghost all in the same sentence.

Does anyone else have this same problem, sometimes I really have to think about which part of the Godhead they are speaking about? Do we really believe in the Trinity Godhead or not?

I believe there are three separate entities that make up the Trinity Godhead, God the Father, God the Son and God the Holy Ghost. We need to be very careful with the statements we make if we are speaking in a leadership position. It is just as easy to speak Gods' word correctly as to speak it incorrectly.

I believe God sent the Holy Ghost to be our teacher and comforter during our everyday lives on this present earth after the death and resurrection of Jesus back to Gods' Throne Room in Heaven as seen in the following scriptures.

In John 14: Jesus talking:

[16] ***And I will pray the Father, and he shall give you another Comforter, that he may abide with you forever;***

[17] *Even the Spirit of truth; whom the world cannot receive, because it seeth him not, neither knoweth him: but ye know him; for he dwelleth with you, and shall be in you.*

[26] *But the Comforter, which is the Holy Ghost, whom the Father will send in my name, he shall teach you all things, and bring all things to your remembrance, whatsoever I have said unto you.*

I believe Jesus and the Holy Ghost are the prominent Godhead entities mentioned in the New Testament but they always acknowledge Father God as the supreme authority and the eternal Creator of Heaven, Earth and mankind as seen in the following scriptures.

Matthew 19:

[16] *And, behold, one came and said unto him,* ***Good*** *Master, what* ***good*** *thing shall I do, that I may have eternal life?*

[17] *And he said unto him, Why callest thou me* ***good****? there is none* ***good*** *but one, that is, God: but if thou wilt enter into life, keep the commandments.*

I believe even in your worst times in life when you cannot see any way out of your heartache and troubles, God always sees what is beautiful and worthy of redemption in you.

I believe God sent Jesus down to our present earth to die for our sins so that we could be redeemed from the curse of sin placed on mankind thru the disobedience of Gods' instructions by Adam and Eve while living in the Garden of Eden.

My question for you today is, where will you spend your final destination, with God or Satan? We need to search our lives and have a made up mind like Joshua in the following scripture.

Joshua 24: [15] *And if it seem evil unto you to serve the LORD, choose you this day whom ye will serve; whether the gods which your fathers served that were on the other side of the flood, or the gods of the Amorites, in whose land ye dwell: but as for me and my house, we will serve the LORD.*

Sometimes we just read thru a scripture and never grasp its true meaning, I call this surface reading. I believe many prophetic events and scriptures are being fulfilled every day that reveals to us the true meaning of Gods' Holy Word.

CHAPTER ONE

OUR PRESENT EARTH

As we begin our journey thru time on our present earth let's begin by visiting **Genesis Chapter One, Verse One,** in our Bibles which states:

In the beginning God created the heaven and the earth.

According to this verse, God created our present earth and it had a beginning.

Mankind has tried to figure out the age of this present earth using man's abilities thru science and astrology but this earth's age is something that only God knows.

God created this present earth many, many years before it was regenerated in the second part of **Verse Two of Genesis Chapter One** when scripture said: *And the spirit of God moved upon the face of the water,* and in the **Third Verse of Genesis Chapter One** which says, *And God said, Let there be light, and there was light:*

Someone ask me the question, where did God come from?

I replied that God did not come from anywhere, He just always was. God is from the spirit world and He was here before the beginning when He created our present material earth that we live on and He will be here when this present material earth is done away with when He creates The New Earth as recorded in Revelation Chapter Twenty One.

The word Heaven **which is singular** in verse one is referring to the location of Gods' Holy City which was located directly above our present earth in the beginning when God created the first Heaven and the earth.

The Holy City of God was clearly visible for all those residing on our present earth at that time which was many of Gods' angels along with the archangel Lucifer whom God had put in charge of the earth.

The atmosphere between our present earth and Gods' Holy City was clean, pure and clear with no stars, clouds or nothing to obscure the visions of Lucifer and those angels who inhabited this present earth from seeing into Gods' Holy City and His Throne Room every day.

God said in verse fourteen let there be lights in this firmament or atmosphere so He created the stars, the moon to light up the night and the sun to light the day which would divide the light from the darkness on our present earth that we now see when we look up.

God created this atmosphere in verse fourteen to block the view of His Holy City from our present earth after the rebellion of the archangel Lucifer and those angels whom he had convinced to follow him in his rebellion against God.

Lucifer began feeling very important in his leadership position. While looking up into Gods' Holy City into Gods' Throne Room day after day he soon became filled with pride and arrogance and decided that he should also have a throne with its location above the stars **(angels)** of God so that he could become equal with God.

God already had a plan to create man who would live on this present earth when He created it in the beginning as seen in the following verse.

Ephesians 1: [4] According as he hath chosen us in him before the foundation of the world, that we should be holy and without blame before him in love:

This verse says that God had already chosen man before the foundation of the world was created.

God was using His angels as caretakers getting our earth ready for mankind to live on it. God did not create man as an afterthought, whim or on a spur of a moment per the above scripture in Ephesians 1: Verse 4.

As we continue this journey let's see what verse two has to say about our present earth: *And the earth was without form, and void; and darkness was upon the face of the deep. We see this* in the following picture.

Why did this present earth become void, dark and without form? The answer is because Lucifer who was later called Satan wanted *to* be omnipotent **(to have all power)**, omnipresent **(to be in all places at the same time)** omniscient **(all knowing)** just like God.

Lucifer had convinced some of the angels living on our present earth to join him in rebelling against God wanting to exalt himself as a god above God.

Lucifer did not care about the eternal fate of these angels, nor does he care about the eternal fate of mankind that he deceives into following him on our present earth by rejecting God and His Son Jesus.

Lucifer is still full of pride and arrogance and he only cares about himself. He is still trying to convince men and women to reject God and Jesus on our present earth today.

I believe Lucifer thought he could actually win in his rebellion against God.

I was discussing this subject with a friend of mine by the name of Cliff who is now resting in the presence of God asleep in Jesus in Paradise located currently in Heaven. Cliff had been the CEO of a number of companies during his lifetime and he stated that in the business world to be totally in charge and able to make the final decisions in a business you have to control at least fifty one percent of the assets of a company.

Lucifer was not a smart CEO. He made a very serious accounting mistake by thinking he had convinced over fifty one percent of the angels into following him in his revolt against God while trying to exalt his throne above God to become equal with God.

Lucifer being an archangel with God given authority apparently did not know the exact number of angels that God had created because angels were ascended and descended between Heaven and Our Present Earth constantly so the one third number that scripture says Lucifer convinced to follow him was not near enough.

Lucifer now called Satan or the devil is still trying on our present earth today to acquire a majority of the people living on this present earth as revenge against God by deceiving and convincing mankind into following him instead of God.

Lucifer will try three more times to become on equal bases to God and I believe he still thinks he can win. What a loser.

The second time Lucifer tried to become equal with God is found in Genesis Chapter Eleven. It was thru a man by the name of Nimrod who we will discuss later in our stories. Nimrod was trying to construct a tower that would reach into heaven and install his god Baal on top of this tower to be on equal basis with our true God.

This religion of Baal was and still is Satan's religion which we will discuss later.

Lucifer will try the third time by using the antichrist, the false prophet and the evil armies of mankind at the battle at Armageddon, the Hebrew reference for Armageddon is Har Megiddon or the region of Megiddo.

Lucifer called Satan or the devil will be trying to defeat Jesus and the armies of heaven at the Battle at Armageddon.

If Lucifer could win this battle by defeating Jesus he could keep Jesus from establishing Gods' earthly Kingdom on our present earth for the One Thousand Year Millennium.

He will not be successful this time either. Reference to this is found in,

Revelation Chapter 16: **[16]** *And he **(talking about Satan working thru the antichrist)** gathered them together into a place called in the Hebrew tongue Armageddon.*

Lucifer will try the fourth time at the conclusion of the One Thousand Year Millennium when he will be loosed from prison for a short season per the scripture below. Three unclean spirits which are the spirits of devils will come out of the mouth of Lucifer the dragon, the antichrist and the false prophet who will go to the nations on earth working miracles trying to convince mankind born during the One Thousand Year Millennium into following Lucifer instead of Jesus. Reference to this is found in Revelation Chapter 16: Verse 13. Lucifer's desire is to become the ruler over mankind who lived thru the seven year tribulation period and the children born to them.

Lucifer still will not be successful and this will be the fourth and final time and scripture states that after this he will be cast alive into the lake of fire and brimstone for ever and ever. Reference to this is found in the following scriptures.

Revelation Chapter 20:

[7] *And when the thousand years are expired, Satan shall be loosed out of his prison,*

[8] *And shall go out to deceive the nations which are in the four quarters of the earth, Gog and Magog, to gather them together to battle: the number of whom is as the sand of the sea.*

[9] *And they went up on the breadth of the earth, and compassed the camp of the saints about, and the beloved city: and fire came down from God out of heaven, and devoured them.*

[10] *And the devil that deceived them was cast into the lake of fire and brimstone, where the beast and the false prophet are, and shall be tormented day and night for ever and ever.*

It is between verses one and two of Genesis Chapter One that Lucifer one of the three archangels mentioned in the Bible rebelled against God and there was a war in the atmosphere between Gods' Holy City and Our Present Earth that we live on.

Lucifer and his armies of angels fought against the armies of God led by Michael another one of Gods' archangels who is the commander of Gods' armies made up of angels.

Lucifer and his army of angels had tried to ascend into Heaven but did not prevail and were cast back down to our present earth.

After this war fought in the atmosphere between Gods' Holy City in Heaven and our present earth, God caused this present earth to become dark, void and without form as punishment and judgment for Lucifer and his army of angels as found in the following scripture.

Jude 1: [6] *And the angels which kept not their first estate* ***(created to serve God),*** *but left their own habitation* ***(on our present earth),*** *he hath reserved in everlasting chains under darkness unto the judgment of the great day* ***(Great White Throne Judgment).***

You might ask the question, why did those angels follow Lucifer in rebelling against God? The answer is Lucifer was and still is the master deceiver and can be very convincing. He probably promised them leadership positions over all the other angels that lived with God in His Holy City.

I ask you the same question today, why does mankind continue to follow Lucifer now called Satan instead of following God even when we have the Holy Scriptures that tells us the fate of Lucifer and all those who will not accept Jesus as their Savior?

I submit the same answer as above. Lucifer is still the master deceiver and is very convincing in his lying to mankind living on our present earth today concerning how great and enjoyable the pleasures of sin are and he is still trying to convince mankind that God doesn't even exist and that Jesus was just an ordinary man who lived and died on earth and is still in the tomb that He was buried in.

A third archangel by the name of Gabriel is Gods' messenger, musician and trumpet blower who in times past delivered Gods' personal instruction to mankind living on earth.

An example of this would be the message delivered to Mary the mother of Jesus by the archangel Gabriel concerning the birth of Jesus.

God will soon instruct Gabriel to sound the last trumpet blast which will signal His coming for the Catching up of the Church to meet Him in the air.

God will than present the Church as the Bride to His Son Jesus the Bridegroom per the following scriptures. This trumpet blast will wake up the dead in Christ asleep in Jesus in Paradise as seen in the below scriptures. What a sound that will be, are you listening?

1Corinthians 15: [52] *In a moment, in the twinkling* ***of an eye****, at the last trump: for the trumpet shall sound, and the dead shall be raised incorruptible, and we shall be changed.*

1Thessalonians 4:

[13] *But I would not have you to be ignorant, brethren, concerning them which are asleep, that ye sorrow not, even as others which have no hope.*

[14] *For if we believe that Jesus died and rose again, even so them also which* ***sleep in Jesus*** *will* <u>**GOD**</u> *bring with him.*

[15] *For this we say unto you by the word of the Lord, that we which are alive and remain unto the coming of the Lord shall not prevent them which are asleep.*

[16] *For the Lord* ***(GOD)*** *himself shall descend from heaven with a shout, with the voice of the archangel, and with the trump of God: and the dead (asleep) in Christ shall rise first:*

[17] *Then we which are alive and remain shall be caught up together with them in the clouds, to meet the Lord in the air: and so shall we ever be with the Lord.*

Are you listening for Gabriel's trumpet blast, I am?

This present earth was completely engulfed by water after Lucifer's rebellion as seen in verse two which states that *the earth was without form, void and darkness was upon the face of the deep, and the spirit of God moved upon the face of the waters.*

God would not and did not create something in the beginning that was void, dark and without form when He created our present earth. It was light, bright and beautiful before the rebellion of Lucifer and the angels who chose to follow him.

Not all of Gods' angels resided on our present earth with Lucifer. Some resided with God in His Holy City located in Heaven. That is why Lucifer made the accounting mistake we talked about above, he had no idea the total number of Gods' angels.

In the following scripture we find God pronouncing judgment on these fallen angels who joined Lucifer in his rebellion against God.

2Peter 2: [4] *For if God spared not the angels that sinned, but cast them down to hell, and delivered them into chains of* ***darkness****, to be* ***reserved*** *unto* ***judgment****;*

Hell called Hades is a place reserved for the unbeliever's spirit who dies in sin who did not and those who will die in the future who will not accept Jesus as their Savior along with the fallen angels mentioned in the above scripture and all will be judged at the Great White Throne Judgment and then cast alive into the Lake of Fire and Brimstone for eternity. This is the second death as described in the Bible in the following scripture.

Revelation 20: [14] *And death and hell were cast into the lake of fire. This is the* ***second death.***

Luke Chapter 16, verses 19 thru 31 refers to Hades as a place for the unbeliever's spirit we just discussed. It is describing the rich man being in Hell or Hades and Lazarus being in the bosom of Abraham called Paradise.

Lucifer due to his pride and lust for power had tried to exalt himself and establish his throne above the Stars of God as seen in the following scriptures in Isaiah.

Isaiah 14:

[13] *For thou* ***(Lucifer)*** *hast said in thine heart, I will ascend into heaven, I will exalt my throne above the stars of God: I will sit also upon the mount of the congregation, in the sides of the north.*

In this verse thirteen it states that Lucifer said in his heart, which was full of pride, that he would ascend into Heaven wanting to exalt his throne above the stars **(angels)** of God.

The above scripture in Isaiah 14: 13 proves that Lucifer had to be living at another location other than heaven when he decided to ascend into Heaven and sit upon the mount of the congregation.

As stated above Lucifer along with many angels resided on our present earth before God caused it to become void, dark and without form after Lucifer's rebellion.

Lucifer had become proud and arrogant, and in verse fourteen of **Isaiah Chapter Fourteen** we can see that his goal was to be like the most High **(GOD).**

[14] *I* ***(Lucifer)*** *will ascend above the heights of the clouds; I will be like the most High.*

God did not destroy this present earth completely, just what was on it.

This present earth has been regenerated two times during the past and will be regenerated one more time in the future since God created it in the beginning.

The first regeneration is found in the second part of **Verse Two of Genesis Chapter One** when it said: *And the spirit of God moved upon the face of the water,* and in the **Third Verse of Genesis Chapter One** which says, *And God said, Let there be light, and there was light:*

At Gods' command our present earth became light and bright again.

Just think about this, history records and gives great credit to a man by the name of Thomas Edison who after trying over one thousand times invented a small object that gave off light that we called the electric light bulb.

In **Verse Three of Genesis Chapter One**, scripture states that God **just spoke a command** and our whole universe became light and bright, a great big bright light bulb.

The second regeneration occurred after the flood during Noah's life while living on our present earth. All living human beings both male, female, animals and plant life had been destroyed by the flood except

Noah and his family a total of eight people along with the animals that God sent for Noah to load onto the Ark.

The third regeneration will occur after the One Thousand Year Millennium when God creates the New Heaven and the New Earth for the saved earthly mankind and the Bride of Christ to live on for eternity.

As we continue our journey on our present earth we read about God creating the first human being, a man, mentioned in our Bible being created by God in Gods' own image and God placing him in a beautiful garden on our present earth to be its caretaker and scripture says he was Gods' earthly friend. God gave him the name of Adam which means red or from the dust of the red earth.

Psalms 144: **[3]** says: *LORD, what is man, that thou takest knowledge of him! or the son of man, that thou makest account of him!*

Some people believe and teach the theory of evolution that mankind evolved from an ape or a monkey but I still believe in the Biblical Creation of man by God as described in the scripture below.

Genesis Chapter 2: **[7]** it says: *And the LORD God formed man* ***(Adam)*** *of the dust of the ground, and breathed into his nostrils the breath of life; and man became a living soul.*

Ladies and gentlemen I submit to you that if man became a living soul, man can also become a dying soul by rejecting Jesus as his or her Savior.

All mankind who have lived on our present earth, past, present and future who rejects Jesus as their Savior will be judged at the Great White Throne Judgment and then be cast into the Lake of Fire for eternity along with Satan (Lucifer), the Antichrist, False Prophet and the fallen angels who chose Lucifer over God per the following scriptures found in:

Revelation Chapter 20.

[11] *And I saw a great white throne, and him* **(GOD)** *that sat on it, from whose face the earth and the heaven fled away; and there was found no place for them.*

[12] *And I saw the dead, small and great, stand before God; and the books were opened: and another book was opened, which is the book of life: and the dead were judged out of those things which were written in the books, according to their works.*

[13] *And the sea gave up the dead which were in it; and death and hell delivered up the dead which were in them: and they were judged every man according to their works.*

[14] *And death and hell were cast into the lake of fire. This is the second death.*

[15] *And whosoever was not found written in the book of life was cast into the lake of fire.*

This judgment is for the unsaved dead and the unsaved who are still alive on earth.

I believe when a Christian dies his or hers saved spirit ascends to rest in Paradise asleep in Jesus until God brings these saved spirits with Him to meet those who are saved and alive on our present earth to be caught up in the air in the catching up of the Church. Some teach that the Church will be judged along with those who are unsaved and all will stand before God at the Great White Throne Judgment but I believe we who are saved have already been judged and found righteous when we accepted Jesus as our Savior and Jesus presented us to Father God as sons and daughters to become heirs and joint heirs with Jesus to live for ever and ever in the Kingdom of God on the New Earth created by God.

As we continue this journey on our present earth scripture states that God created a beautiful garden with many species of animals and birds to live on land and many sea creatures to live in the bodies of water located on our present earth both male and female for Adam to care for and watch over.

God gave Adam the opportunity to give a name to each and every one of the animals both male and female but God created only one human being, the man Adam.

As our journey on our present earth continues we find God descending down one day into this beautiful garden from His throne room in Heaven to visit and fellowship with Adam in the cool of the afternoon as He often did.

On this day God noticed that Adam had a very sad and different look in his eyes which He had never noticed before.

God thought, I know what is wrong with Adam, he's lonely, so this is what I am going to do. I will put Adam into a deep sleep and I will remove a small rib from his ribcage nearest to his heart which I will use to create a female helper for him.

Genesis 2: [21] *And the LORD God caused a deep sleep to fall upon Adam and he slept: and he took one of his ribs, and closed up the flesh instead thereof;*

Ladies you were not created by God to be a slave for man. You were created to be a helper or help meet for man, not under his feet or over his head and certainly not his slave.

Men this is not my words but Gods' word. Take care of your lady and treat her with respect.

On this day instead of talking and visiting with Adam as He usually did, God caused Adam to fall into a deep sleep while performing an operation on him.

The Bible does not record how long it took to complete this operation or how long Adam was asleep during his recovery time but when Adam woke up what a surprise, surprise, surprise there was in store for him.

Adam setting up began blinking and rubbing his eyes trying to clear the sleep from his eyes trying to wake up not believing what he was seeing still thinking that maybe he was asleep and dreaming.

Adams saw this beautiful creature and his first though was, am I still asleep and dreaming, I sure hope not. He probably pinched himself to make sure he was actually awake.

Adam had never seen a creature so beautiful. Just looking at her took Adam's breath completely away and she smelled so good and fresh and all he could mutter was wo-man.

There in his home was this gorgeous creature with big round beautiful eyes and long flowing locks of hair walking around in his home and she was conversing with him using the same language that God had taught him to speak when he communicated with God and the animals.

Adam's immediate thought was, WOW, I wonder who she is and where she came from.

Adam's mind was whirling, he was having trouble breathing. His heart was pounding and beating so hard that he thought it might burst at any moment and he was so nervous and excited and all he could say was wo-man, wo-man, and wo-man.

I wonder if Adam was talking to himself trying to calm down his emotions until he could get himself under control or was he talking to this beautiful creature when he uttered the word wo-man.

Maybe Adam was saying wow-man but in his excitement it came out wo-man. What do you think?

Whichever it was, I think Adam was very nervous and excited.

Have you ever wondered what this beautiful lady might have been thinking, I have?

She had never seen a man before in her life. In fact she had never seen anything before in her life until just a few minutes ago when God created her using one of Adam's ribs as a starting point to build her body around and then God breathed His breath of life into her and woke her up.

She had just been created by God into existence, perfect in every way, not one blemish, the future mother of all mankind, so everything she was seeing and experiencing was new to her.

Adam had never seen a female creature like this before. All the other animals and creatures living in the garden that God had created walked around on four legs and most were very hairy and sometimes very smelly.

This one was walking upright on two legs just like Adam and she was so gorgeous and beautiful and what a wonderful sweet fragrance kept coming into Adams' nostrils as he began to breathe deeply, deeply and more deeply while he continued to utter wo-man or wow-man.

No sinus problems, allergies or stuffy nose for Adam on this day.

So Adam still not believing what he was seeing and still a little shook up thought, I wonder who she is and where she came from and where she is going. I sure like the looks of this creature more than all those other creatures living in this garden. I sure would like to know more about her. I wonder what her name is. Adam's mind was so full of questions.

Adam finally getting his composure and emotions somewhat under control introduced himself to her and told her that his name was Adam and that God had built him this beautiful home many years ago and had made him the caretaker of this beautiful garden with lots of animals living in it.

Of course this beautiful female creature did not know what he meant when he said home, garden or animals and she had only seen God once when He woke her up and she did not really know who God was.

She had never seen a house, garden or an animal because she had just been created by God and had never even been outdoors.

Adam still very excited asked her if she had time to stay and visit for a while and if she was hungry he would fix her something to eat.

Think about it, this lady had never had anything to eat in her life since she was only a few hours old. Eating would be a totally new experience for her.

She thought I like talking to Adam and after looking around thought what a beautiful home Adam has and this God that he talks about must really like him.

Adam who was the first master chef to live on our present earth and wanting to make a good impression on her decided that he would fix a gourmet meal for her since she had consented to stay for a while.

This garden where Adam lived had an abundance of different fruits and vegetables growing in it, so Adam hurriedly gathered some fresh fruits and vegetables and began to prepare a gourmet meal for her.

By this time it was getting very late in the afternoon and the sun was starting to go down in the west and soon it would become very dark outside.

Adam was enjoying being and visiting with this female creature so much by this time that he started searching the memory banks of his mind trying to think of something or anything he could say that would keep her from leaving.

Adam being the perfect gentleman informed her that she should not be wandering around in the dark of the night by herself. This female creature being very polite agreed since she did not know what Adam was talking about when he said she should not be wandering around in the dark of the night.

Remember she had just been created a few hours before during the warm sunshine of the afternoon and had never seen or experienced darkness.

Adam enjoyed visiting and talking with God when He came down to visit and fellowship with him and God always talked back with Adam but God only visited in the cool of the afternoon. Adam never had anyone to talk to during the morning time or the night time after God returned to His

Holy City except the animals and when Adam talked with the animals it was mostly a one sided conversation.

Adam still very excited thought I am sure going to enjoy visiting and talking with this lady some more.

Ladies and gentlemen I believe old Adam is love struck, don't you?

Adam was so excited and intrigued with this new female creature that he never remembered that just a few hours before she showed up in his home he had felt so sad, lonely and all alone.

Ladies and gentlemen just remember if you start feeling sad and all alone during your life while living on our present earth that God is still there for you. Just talk to God using your everyday language and I can guarantee that you will feel much better soon.

Adam thought my life in this garden is getting better.

So after dinner and having gotten his emotions under control and being the perfect gentlemen, Adam asked this beautiful female creature her name and enquired as to where she lived and where she was going before showing up in his home.

Of course this beautiful creature had no idea how to answer Adam. She did not have a name and she had nowhere to go since God had just created her a few hours before during the afternoon, so she just replied:

Oh someone just dropped me off in the neighborhood and I thought I would come in and visit for a while.

Good answer, don't you think, but perfectly true, God had just dropped her off?

Adam had no idea that God had just created her because he had just woke up from a deep sleep and there she was standing and walking around in his house.

Adam did not know that he had just gone thru an operation and was one rib short. He was not even sore. God had done a great surgical job on Adam leaving no incision whatsoever for Adam to see or to recover from.

A friend of mine told me that this rib taken from Adam contained most all of the emotions found in the human body. He said that is the reason women are more emotional than men. What do you think could this be true or not?

Ladies and gentlemen this was the first medical operation recorded on this present earth and it was performed by God the Great Physician maybe on the kitchen table in Adam's home.

What an exciting first day on our present earth this beautiful female creature was experiencing.

Since God had given Adam the privilege of giving a name to all the other animals and creatures on earth, Adam thinking to himself said, what name can I give to this beautiful creature?

Adam being a very creative man and wanting to give her a very special name thought, I know, I will call her Eve which is short for evening since she just dropped in for a visit in the cool of the afternoon. I think Adam was very creative, don't you?

Eve became very excited and happy to finally know her name and she talked with Adam all night and into the next day.

No sleep that night for either of them, but remember Adam had been in a deep, deep sleep all day long. He sure wasn't sleepy and Eve had just been created so she wasn't sleepy either.

In fact everything Eve was experiencing during this first day and night on our present earth was new to her so she did not know that people went to sleep or what was meant by going to sleep.

Adam and Eve talked more the next day and continued talking day after day and soon they were inseparable and both madly in love with each other.

I think this was love at first sight for Adam when he first saw her in his home.

Adam thought, life in this garden is getting better and better in fact I'm beginning to love my life more and more.

Since Adam had been enjoying her company so much during the last few days he ask Eve if she would consider staying for a while and living in the garden. Adam informed her that he would be glad to construct another home just for her near the house that God had built for him.

Eve agreed to stay for a while and to live in the garden. She had not told Adam that she had nowhere else to go anyway, so she was happy to have a place to call home and be able to live in this beautiful garden with Adam.

Adam thought life living in this garden is getting better and better and better.

God continued coming down every day during the cool of the afternoon to fellowship and talk with Adam and Eve discussing what they had been doing and experiencing on our present earth.

God thought, Adam seems very happy and he does not have that sad and lonely look in his eyes anymore.

Adam being very proud of Eve was so excited to show her all thru this beautiful garden and he introduced her to all the creatures and animals living in the garden that God had created.

Eve loved eating the fruits and vegetables found in the garden and meeting, talking and petting all the animals and soon all the animals loved Eve.

Adam also informed Eve what God had told him about not looking at or eating from the tree in the mist of the garden called The Tree of Knowledge of Good and Evil.

Adam thought, God has sure been good to me and my life is just wonderful. I wonder what God has in store for me in the future.

If Adam had only known what his future was going to entail, I am sure his life would have turned out very differently and this story would have had a very different ending for us to read about in the Bible.

I'm sure just like Adam we all can say that God has been very good to each and every one of us during our life time on this present earth.

If God has been good to you, why don't you just stop what you are doing and give Him praise and thanks now.

A few days later being so in love and being inseparable, Adam very graciously asked Eve if she would consider becoming his wife and helper in life and she gladly accepted his proposal.

After the marriage ceremony which was officiated by God with a lot of animals in attendance, Adam and Eve became the first human family ever recorded as living on our present earth.

What a beautiful place God had provided for them to live and enjoy.

God named it the Garden of Eden.

Gods' creation was perfect. Adam & Eve were created to live forever in the Garden of Eden, raising a family and enjoying living on our present earth. They were so happy and so in love.

During Adam's life living in the garden, there was no measurement of time in years as we know it today. Adam never aged during his time living in the garden. Adam's life recorded by years started when he and Eve were banished from the garden as we will discuss in our story soon.

Adam thought my life living in this garden has gotten better and better and better and better.

One day near mid-morning Eve informed Adam that she was going to go gather some vegetables and fruit to fix for their lunch and ask him if he wanted to come along.

Adam must have taught Eve how to cook since she had just been created a few weeks before and did not know anything about eating and cooking. Maybe cooking just came natural to Eve, what do you think?

Adam yawning a very big yawn replied that he was really tired. Adam told Eve that he had worked very hard the day before tending to the animals and sprucing up the garden and decided that he would just stay home and relax for a while in his recliner and maybe take a nap before time for God to come down to visit them as He always did in the cool of the afternoon.

While gathering food for lunch Eve met a creature that she had never seen before in this beautiful Garden of Eden and when this creature spoke to her she could understand its speech. Adam had never introduced this creature to Eve. It was not like any of the other animals that Adam had introduced to her. This creature walked on two legs just like Adam and Eve and spoke very fluently and was very mannerly.

Since Eve had never seen this creature in the garden before, she became very excited and asked the creature, where do you live and what is your name?

The creature replied that his name was Lucifer and that he and his family lived beyond the mountains in the land south of this garden and that most of his family lived in very comfortable underground homes where the temperature remained the same all year long and invited her to come for a visit some time.

Lucifer, the devil or Satan as he is called today has used many different disguises to tempt mankind all thru the ages just as he did Eve this day in the Garden of Eden and he is still doing the same to mankind today on our present earth.

Some people picture him as a little red devil with horns and a pitchfork in his hand but I can assure you that this is not the form that he uses when he comes to tempt and to deceive mankind.

Lucifer informed Eve that this was the first time he had ventured so far from his homeland so when he saw the beautiful green lush garden he just had to stop and check it out.

He said his homeland was very dark, hot and smelly, not green, lush and cool like the garden where she lived. Very different from what he had just told her a few minutes before in describing his home as being a very comfortable place to live where the temperature was always the same and had invited her to come for a visit.

Ladies and gentlemen beware of listening to the words of Satan. He will use just enough of the truth to disguise his evil ways and change his stories many times trying to deceive you and he never tells the full truth only half truths in his deceptions.

Lucifer told Eve that he had no idea that anyone lived in this garden or that it even existed. In fact he said that he had never talked to or seen a human being before.

This was not the whole truth as we will see a little later on concerning the Tree of Knowledge.

Eve informed Lucifer that her husband Adam was home resting but she was sure Adam would love to meet him.

During their conversation Lucifer told Eve that once upon a time he had access to a beautiful city far away in Heaven with a ruler by the name of Jehovah God which had many servants that He calls angels.

He told Eve that he had been a beautiful archangel and that he had been put in charge of Jehovah Gods' angels living on this present earth.

When Eve asked Lucifer why he did not have access to Heaven anymore and now lived on this present earth, he replied with a little sarcasm in his voice that when angels like him get old and reach retirement age that Jehovah God requires them to retire from their duties and sends them to live on earth permanently just like He had done to Lucifer and his angel friends.

Eve being very gullible was starting to feel very sorry for Lucifer and was about to invite him to come and have lunch with her and Adam but before she could ask, Lucifer had changed the conversation to another subject.

Lucifer had looked at the vegetables and fruits that Eve had gathered in her basket and then asked if she had ever eaten fruit from the Tree of Knowledge located in the middle of the garden?

Lucifer said the fruit from that tree was so beautiful to look at and it was so good, juicy and flavorful to eat.

Eve being so excited about meeting and talking with Lucifer and wanting to introduce him to Adam that she never thought to ask how he knew about the tree in the middle of the garden since he had just told her a little while ago that this was his first time to visit this garden.

Lucifer is such a smooth talker so how will you know when he is lying? It happens as soon as he opens his mouth?

Eve replied to Lucifer that God had instructed her husband Adam to not eat fruit from that tree or even to look upon it. Adam had told her to stay away from it because if they ate of its fruit or even looked upon it God had said they would surely die.

Lucifer began laughing so hard that soon his eyes were watering with tears rolling down his checks replied, you know, Jehovah God has not changed at all. He still wants everyone to think that He is still the supreme authority, always in charge, telling you what to do and how to do it and telling you that you will die if you eat the fruit from that tree. You will not die, you will only acquire a lot of knowledge and be just like Jehovah God and He doesn't want you to become as intelligent as He is.

Jehovah God wants that fruit for Himself and the angels that live with him. That's His personal favorite fruit tree and He loves the fruit from that tree more than all the other fruit in the garden because it's so beautiful to look at and so good, juicy and tasty.

Eve though, maybe Lucifer is right, maybe that is why God doesn't want us to eat fruit from that tree since we would become as intelligent as He is and it's His favorite tree.

Lucifer was so convincing that soon Eve was convinced that was why God told Adam to not eat the fruit from that tree.

Lucifer told Eve that God would never know or even care if she just experience a little taste of that fruit and would never even miss any of the fruit from that tree since God only came down to the garden in the cool of the afternoon to visit them and gather fruit from this tree and besides that fruit grows back very quickly.

In Gods' eyes a little taste of sin is sin there is no little sins or big sins.

Eve never thought to ask Lucifer how he knew that God came down to visit them in the cool of the afternoon since he had just told her a little while ago that this was his first time to visit the garden. Just another one of Satan's lies.

Satan is very good at starting little doubting thoughts in our mind trying to get us confused just as he did to Eve. When he does this, we need to quickly rebuke and resist him in the Name of Jesus and God instead of listening to him.

The following verse says that he will flee from us if we will quickly rebuke and resist him.

James 4: [7] *Submit yourselves therefore to God.* ***Resist the devil****, and he will flee from you.*

Lucifer knowing he had gotten Eve's full attention said, come on with me and I will show you that the fruit on that tree is awesome.

Lucifer was so convincing that soon Eve was following him to the tree in the middle of the garden and after looking at the beautiful ripe fruit she begin picking some of the fruit and began to eat.

Just as Lucifer said, it was so good, juicy and tasty. As soon as she ate the fruit it gave her energy and knowledge that she had never experienced before. Everything around her looked so much brighter and she seemed to know more about life than ever before and she was still alive, she did not die as God said she would.

Before long Adam waking up from his nap and looking up at the position of the sun realized that Eve had been gone a long time. Adam began to get worried about her and decided to go looking for her. Adam was so relieved when he saw his beautiful Eve walking toward him from the middle of the garden.

Eve seeing Adam realizing that she had been gone a long time quickly ran toward Adam giving him a big hug and ask him if he was hungry and when he replied that he sure was Eve reached into her basket and gave Adam some of the fruit that she had picked from the Tree of Knowledge of Good and Evil to eat as a snack before lunch.

Immediately both their minds became quick in understanding and knowledge of life both good and evil.

They looked at each other in amazement and for the first time realized that they were naked and started looking for something to cover up with. They could only find some fig leaves that were big enough to cover themselves up with.

Holiness is pure and shameless but sin always requires a cover up.

Just before Adam found Eve in the middle of the garden, Lucifer had informed Eve that he was late for another appointment and was long gone before Adam showed up.

Lucifer promised Eve before he departed that he would come back soon to visit her and Adam. This is one time that Lucifer told the truth as we will discuss later in our story.

Soon God descended from His throne room in heaven into the Garden of Eden to visit with them in the cool of the afternoon but they were nowhere to be found.

God called out, Adam, Adam where are you? Adam replied very weakly over here.

God found them hiding amongst the foliage growing in the garden and when He ask Adam why they were hiding, Adam told him about eating the fruit that Eve had given him to eat from the Tree of Knowledge of Good and Evil and he blamed Eve for giving him the fruit to eat.

God turned to Eve asking, what have you done? Eve told God about her earlier meeting and visiting with Lucifer and blamed Lucifer for deceiving her into eating from the tree.

Later when God confronted Lucifer he just smiled and blamed God for sending him to live on this present earth.

No one accepted responsibility for their disobedience of God's instructions just as a lot of people are not accepting responsibility for living in sin today always blaming someone else for their sins.

Due to the temptation and deceitfulness of Eve by Lucifer, both Adam and Eve by eating the fruit from the Tree of Knowledge had let sin come into their lives by listening to Lucifer instead of trusting God and obeying His instructions to not look at or eat from the tree of Knowledge of Good and Evil.

For their disobedience of Gods' instructions, they had to be removed quickly from this beautiful garden that God had created for them to live in.

God removed them from the Garden of Eden before Lucifer who was later called Satan could come back to convince them into eating from the Tree of Life as spoken in,

Verse Twenty Two of Genesis Chapter Three which says: *And the LORD God said, Behold, the man is become as one of us* ***(Father, Son and Holy Ghost the Trinity Godhead)****, to know good and evil: and now, lest he put forth his hand, and take also of the tree of life, and eat, and live forever.*

If Adam and Eve had eaten fruit from the Tree of Life they would have lived forever with sin in their lives. At that time they had only eaten fruit from the Tree of Knowledge of Good and Evil which God had instructed them not to eat from. By doing so they did acquire the knowledge of good and evil but now had the curse of sin in their lives.

The Word of God states that after God removed Adam and Eve from the Garden of Eden that He placed Cherubim's with flaming swords to guard the entrances to the Garden of Eden to prevent Lucifer or anyone else from ever entering into this beautiful garden again.

The New Earth that God will create for us to live on and enjoy after the One Thousand Year Millennium is over as described in the book of Revelation Chapter 21 will be just like the Garden of Eden with green foliage, flowers, beautiful trees and once again watered from below the earth's surface.

God has given to each of us a free will to make a choice just like He did Adam and Eve. God simply ask each of us the following question.

Whom do you choose to serve today Me or Satan?

Have you made this decision today, if not please make the correct choice today by choosing to serve God instead of choosing to serve Satan. There is no middle ground; your choice will be either God or Satan.

I believe the Garden of Eden was probably located in the Nation of Iraq on this present earth due to reading scriptures in the Bible and thru my studies from other sources. Just my personal belief but wherever the location, this beautiful garden had gorgeous flowers, trees, lots of animals and food in abundance.

Adam and Eve had everything their hearts and lives desired while living in the Garden of Eden. They just listened to the wrong creature Lucifer and had to be removed from this garden and it cost them everything.

Men and women living on our present earth today are still listening and being deceived by Lucifer now called Satan or the devil and are losing their lives just like Adam and Eve did and they will be rewarded to live in the Lake of Fire and brimstone for eternity.

Ladies and gentlemen listen to God, read His word and accept Jesus as your Savior and you will inherit eternal life and have the opportunity to live on God's New Earth soon to be created.

There was only one thing that God had instructed Adam to not do while living in this beautiful garden and that was to not look at, touch or eat from the tree in the mist of the garden called the Tree of Knowledge of Good and Evil.

Have you noticed that when we humans are told not to do something that we just cannot wait to do it? Some calls this human nature. God did not create Adam and Eve with human nature when He created them.

Adam and Eve were created with a Godly nature given by God Himself. Human nature was acquired thru Lucifer when Adam and Eve disobeyed the instructions of God and chose to follow Lucifer instead of God.

They listened to the wrong creature Lucifer who is now called Satan or the devil and soon due to Lucifer's convincing temptation's, Eve had looked upon this tree and saw that it had beautiful fruit for the eye to look upon and so appealing to the appetite.

Sin is always appealing to mortal men and women and sometimes it is beautiful to look upon. Just because it is appealing and beautiful does not make it the correct choice for mankind just as Adam and Eve soon found out.

In Romans 6: 23 it says: *For the wages* ***(reward)*** *of sin is death but the gift of God is eternal life with Jesus Christ our Lord.*

Salvation is a gift from God made available to us thru the death of His Son Jesus. It cannot be purchased with good works as some believe but is a gift received by faith unto salvation thru the shed blood of Jesus that covers all our sins.

Eve had picked and ate some of the fruit before she gave some to Adam to eat for a snack before lunch as any loving wife who prepares food for her husband.

Only one problem, God had told Adam to not eat from this forbidden tree but just like many husbands on our present earth today we want to please our wives and will usually eat any food that they prepare and just like Adam we never ask the question, where did this food come from?

Men we know that eating the food prepared by our wives and thanking them for cooking for us is our way of showing love for our spouses. This will also keep peace in our homes so men never compare your wife's cooking to someone else's. That is a big no, no.

Adam was so in love with his beautiful Eve that God had given to him that he had eaten the fruit that she gave him from the Tree of Knowledge of Good and Evil before he thought about the consequences they would suffer.

Do you think Adam knew where the fruit came from? I personally don't know the answer that question, but I do know that we still have to give an account to God for our sins just as Adam was required to do.

Have you ever wondered what would have happened if Adam and Eve would have just admitted to God their sin and ask God to forgive them immediately?

I personally think God would have forgiven them immediately but they did not ask God for forgiveness but each one blamed someone else for their sins as we discussed above so God removed them from living in the garden.

Adam and Eve paid a high price for their disobedience and were expelled from this beautiful Garden of Eden which was located on our present earth.

Lucifer a fallen archangel who was a spirit being also paid a price for his part in deceiving Eve into eating from this tree. For his judgment he will be required to spend eternity in the Lake of Fire with others who have rejected God and Jesus.

God told the serpent which had allowed Lucifer to use and disguise his body that from now on you will crawl upon your belly and eat the dust of this present earth all the days of your life and all people who see you will call you a serpent or a snake.

You see Lucifer did not have a physical body and could not be seen because he was and still is a spirit being. He needed a physical body to inhabit and work thru so he chose and convinced the serpent to let him use his earthly body.

He still needs an earthly human body to work thru don't let him use yours.

I don't think this serpent looked like a snake or crawled upon his belly until God pronounced judgment on him for allowing Lucifer to use his body as seen in the following scripture.

Genesis 3: [14] *And the LORD God said unto the serpent, Because thou hast done this, thou art cursed above all cattle, and above every beast of the field; upon thy belly shalt thou go, and dust shalt thou eat all the days of thy life:*

In this scripture, God was talking to the serpent not to Lucifer.

God will pronounce judgment at the Great White Throne Judgment for all mankind who lets Lucifer now called Satan use their bodies on our present earth.

Adam and Eve could have lived forever in this beautiful garden on our present earth but due to the deceitfulness by Satan they would now have to work by the sweat of their brow to obtain food for their family to eat.

This may have caused the first fight between a husband and wife living on our present earth or a least a huge disagreement but due to Adam being so in love with Eve and looking into those big round beautiful eyes of hers filling up with teardrops his heart melted and he soon forgave her.

I imagine that it was a long time before Adam had any desire to eat fruit again. He was probably a meat and vegetable man for a long time after being removed from the Garden of Eden, what do you think?

God never changes His word or plans and He had told Adam that he would surely die if he ate the fruit from the Tree of Knowledge of good and evil. Due to Lucifer's deceitfulness both Adam and Eve did spiritually die immediately but they would also suffer a physical death at a later time.

God also told Eve that she would suffer labor pains during child birth for her disobedience, so now ladies you know the rest of the story as Paul Harvey used to say.

I believe Adam and Eve repented and asked God for forgiveness many times after being expelled from the garden before they experienced their physical death on our present earth.

Now Adam finds himself in the role of a farmer. He has to till the ground to raise food for his family. The days were long and hot unlike the cool days he enjoyed in the Garden of Eden. Not only was this present earth's soil hard to till but thistles, thorns and other weeds grew much faster than the plants and seeds he was planting to raise food for his family.

I am sure that Adam and Eve would encounter a snake every now and then while working on the farm which would remind them of the life that they had given up in the Garden of Eden due to their disobedience to God and this would go on for the remainder of their lives.

As time went on Adam and Eve had a beautiful baby boy and they named him Cain. Cain like his father grew up to be a farmer following in the footsteps of Adam.

Adam was so proud to have a son who wanted to be just like dad. Soon Adam and Eve were blessed with another little bundle of joy, another little baby boy and they named him Abel. Abel became a rancher because he loved to raise sheep, goats and other animals.

One day as these boys were growing older the subject of God entered into their conversation so they decided to offer God a sacrifice to see if He would bless their lives. I'm sure they had listened to Adam and Eve discussing God and how they were blessed while living in the Garden of Eden.

The Bible does not say this but I am sure that these two boys were just like boys in today's society on our present earth. They had inquisitive minds and had asked Adam and Eve many times why they had moved from the Garden of Eden if it was so beautiful with lots of food in abundance.

Adam and Eve as parents probably did not want to tell the boy's why they had to leave the beautiful Garden of Eden or what had happened. They might have said something like this, oh we just wanted to move on and experience new adventures and a new life in a new country.

There was just one problem with Cain's sacrifice. Cain decided that it did not matter what he brought as a sacrifice to God just so he brought something to offer as a sacrifice.

This is just like a lot of Christians today who only serve God half heartily and only when it fits their life style. If you are one of these type of Christians, God may not invite you to live with Him on His New Earth just as He did not accept Cain's sacrifice. Something to think about.

Abel on the other hand brought a firstborn lamb from his sheep herd, a lamb without blemish for a sacrifice and Abel's sacrifice pleased God very much.

When God comes for the Church as the Bride for His Son Jesus, He will not accept a blemished Bride. Church we need to get ready and get our act together.

God's word states that without a blood sacrifice there is no redemption for sin. This is why Jesus died on the cross and shed his blood while living on our present earth and offered Himself as the total sacrifice for all mankind to have the opportunity to be saved.

Today on our present earth to receive the gift of salvation by grace all we have to do is believe in our hearts that Jesus is the Son of God and that He died on the cross for our sins and repent and ask forgiveness for our sins and God will forgive us and blot out our sins covered by the blood of His Son Jesus.

God was not pleased with Cain's mediocre sacrifice so He rejected Cain's offering which made Cain very angry so Cain took his anger out on his brother Abel.

I can just hear Cain in his fit of anger swearing, screaming and telling Abel that he was the favorite son of Adam and Eve and they liked Abel much more than him and during his fit of anger he struck and killed his brother Abel and buried his body.

Remember when I stated above that Lucifer promised Eve that day in the garden that he would come and visit her and Adam again, guess what, the day their son Cain killed his brother Abel, Lucifer kept his promise.

What Cain did not realize was that God see's all and knows all so when God ask Cain about his brother Abel, Cain replied, am I my brother's keeper? God told Cain that Abel's blood was calling out to Him from the ground.

Numbers 32: [23] *But if ye will not do so* ***(repent),*** *behold, ye have sinned against the LORD: and be sure your sin will* ***find you out****.*

Cain knew that all the people living around him would soon realize that he had killed his brother Abel and would try to kill him in revenge and soon he would become a fugitive and a vagabond on this present earth so he asked God to protect him from those living around him. This was a selfish request not a request for forgiveness, just a request to disguise him from all who knew him.

Scripture states in **Verse Fifteen of Genesis Chapter Four** that God in His mercy placed a mark on Cain to disguise and protect him from all who would try to kill him for killing his brother Abel. God see's each and every one of us today in our natural lives, are we pleasing to God?

During the seven years of the tribulation end time period on this present earth, the devil working thru the antichrist will try to force all mankind living on our present earth to receive his special mark for anyone to be able to buy or sell. If you receive this special mark called the Mark of the Beast showing your allegiance to Satan called the devil in scripture there will be no forgiveness for your sins and you will spend eternity with Satan in the Lake of Fire.

We need to be very careful as to what we do and say because the scripture's states that we will give an account for our actions as seen in the following scriptures.

Matthew 12: [36] *But I say unto you, that every idle word that men shall speak, they shall give account thereof in the day of judgment.*

Romans 14: [**12**] *So then every one of us shall* ***give account*** *of himself to God.*

Hebrews 13: [**17**] *Obey them that have the rule over you, and submit yourselves: for they watch for your souls, as they that must* ***give account****, that they may do it with joy, and not with grief: for that is unprofitable for you.*

1Peter 4: [**5**] *Who shall* ***give account*** *to him that is ready to judge the quick and the dead.*

Soon Cain and his wife decided that it would be best if they left their current homeland and moved to another country since everyone in their current homeland knew that he had killed his brother Abel.

Per Cain's request, God placed a mark on him so that no one would recognize him. Cain and his wife journeyed to a land called Nod and started their own family and soon had a baby boy by the name of Enoch and scripture says Cain built a city and named it after his son Enoch.

This is not the same Enoch who was a descendant of Seth the third son of Adam and Eve that we will discuss below.

Adam and Eve found themselves very lonely with no children remaining at home after Cain and his family moved away.

God had not forgotten Adam and Eve and soon God blessed them with another little baby boy and they called his name Seth. Seth lived a total of nine hundred and twelve years. After Seth grew up and had his own family he had a son by the name of Enos.

Scripture states that during the lifetime of Enos who lived nine hundred and five years was when men really began to call upon God again.

After Enos reached manhood and had children of his own he had a descendent by the name of Jared who had a son by the name of Enoch. Enoch lived three hundred and sixty five years and the scriptures states that God took Enoch because God found him to be a righteous man.

The Bible does not give the location where God took Enoch but I believe God took Enoch to Paradise located at that time in the center of the earth but now Enoch is in the presence of God asleep in Jesus in Paradise located in heaven awaiting the Catching up of the Church along with all other saints who have died in Christ.

Adam lived a total of nine hundred and thirty years and died after being expelled from the Garden of Eden and experienced a physical death just as God told him he would if he ate from the Tree of Knowledge of Good and Evil in the Garden of Eden.

If Adam and Eve had not sinned by disobeying Gods' instructions they could have lived forever in the Garden of Eden because they had no sin in their lives until they disobeyed God. The measurement of life of mankind being recorded by years started when Adam and Eve were expelled from the Garden of Eden.

God word and plans never change and what He says will come true, and will come to pass, sometimes quickly and sometimes at a later time just like it did Adam which took approximately nine hundred and thirty years to come to pass.

The stories that I chose to write about which are recorded in the Bible talks a lot about the men of that day and time. We have and will discuss some prominent women such as Eve, Sarah, Hannah, Ruth and others during our journey on our present earth because there are some very important stories of women recorded in the Bible that God used to do His will.

Due to man's longevity of life during that period in time living on our present earth scripture records that there were sons and daughters born to mankind on this present earth and scripture states that Cain had a wife. If you are wondering about where Cain's wife came from or who was her father, the bible just does not say.

Somethings are not recorded in our bible because God must have decided that we just did not need to know these people and He just wants us to accept what He said in the scriptures by faith as being true and correct. This is what I have decided to do in my studies of Gods' word and not question His motives.

We Christians today should strive to live our lives so that God can see the righteousness of His Son Jesus in us per the following scripture found in:

Matthew 6: [33] *But seek ye first the kingdom of God, and his righteousness* ***(Jesus Christ)****; and all these things* ***(both spiritual and material)*** *shall be added unto you.*

I was praying and meditating on this scripture and God pressed into my spirit that in this scripture His righteousness is referring to His Son Jesus. God wants us to seek Jesus as our Savior because He is the righteousness of God. If you have not done this, please do so today because tomorrow may be too late.

Back to our story of Enoch we find Enoch had a son by the name of Methuselah who lived nine hundred and sixty nine years, the oldest man to ever live on our present earth as recorded in bible history.

Methuselah had a son by the name of Noah which I am sure all my readers have read or heard about his story and you will recognize him as the man who built the first boat on our present earth called an Ark.

The Bible states that it was during Noah's time that men began to multiply mightily on our present earth and wickedness was increasing greatly and every imagination of the thoughts of man's heart was on evil continually.

Soon the magnitude of man's sins caught the attention of God and God pronounced judgment on mankind and our present earth for the sins of mankind.

This wickedness was partially due to the intermarriages of the sons of God with the daughters of men found in **Genesis Chapter Six, Verses One thru Three.**

[1] *And it came to pass, when men began to multiply on the face of the earth, and daughters were born unto them,*

[2] *That the sons of God saw the daughters of men that they were fair; and they took them wives of all which they chose.*

[3] *And the LORD said, My spirit shall not always strive with man, for that he also is flesh: yet his days shall be an hundred and twenty years.*

In verse three God said that His spirit would not always strive with man and that man was flesh. If these sons of God were angel's as some teach, God would not have called them man that was flesh. I believe God knew who these sons were and would have known the difference between angels and man.

I have heard discussions saying that these sons of God were some of the fallen angels who followed Satan in his rebellion against God but Jesus taught that angels do not marry nor are given in marriage as seen in **Matthew 22: Verse: [30]** *For in the resurrection* ***(talking about the saints)*** *they neither marry, nor are given in marriage, but are as the angels of God in heaven.*

Angels do not marry so they cannot reproduce so these sons of God were not some of the fallen angels as some believe and teach. These sons of God were capable of producing children, angels are not.

Let's look at the following scriptures:

2Peter 2:[4] *For if God spared not the angels that sinned, but cast them down to hell, and delivered them into chains of darkness,* ***to be reserved unto judgment;***

Jude 1: [6] *And the angels which kept not their first estate, but left their own habitation, he hath reserved in everlasting chains under darkness unto the judgment of the great day.*

These sons of God cannot be fallen angels per the above scriptures which states that God delivered them, talking about the fallen angels and reserved them in everlasting chains under darkness to be reserved unto the judgment of the great day talking about the Great White Throne Judgment.

Nowhere in scripture can I find where these fallen angels were ever loosed from their chains of darkness. They are still chained in darkness waiting to be judged and reserved until judgment at the Great White Throne Judgment.

I submit to you that these sons of God were the ungodly descendants of Cain, Adam's first son who intermarried with the daughters of the godly descendants of Seth who was Adam's third son.

It states in Genesis Chapter 4 verse 16 that Cain went out from the presence of the Lord. This intermarriage brought about the judgment of God upon mankind who lived on this present earth during Noah's time.

To confirm my statement above we find in the following verse that Adam was called the son of God, so Adam's son's Cain and Seth would also be called the sons of God.

In Luke 3: [38] *Which was the son of Enos, which was the son of Seth, which was the son of Adam, which was the son of God.*

Remember it was Cain who slew his brother Abel. God does not and will not forget the sins committed by ungodly men and women. I find no place in scripture where Cain ever repented and ask God for forgiveness for his sin of killing his brother Abel.

Just as Adam hid himself from God after eating from the Tree of Knowledge of good and evil, Cain in verse fourteen of Genesis 4 says from thy face **(talking about God)** shall I be hid and be a fugitive and vagabond in the earth.

Today on our present earth men and women are living their lives just like the people were during Noah's time. Sin is ramped everywhere with the imagination of man's heart on evil continually.

I believe the magnitude of this present earth's sins is getting the attention of God and soon He will pronounce judgment on this earth and mankind once again during the Seven Year Tribulation Period found in the last book of our Bible, the Book of Revelation.

God will once again say enough is enough and declare that He is tired of the sins of mankind committed on this present earth that He created just as He did during Noah's time.

God sent His Son to live and die on this present earth so that mankind would have a way to receive forgiveness for their sins but mankind rejected and killed His son after only thirty three years and mankind is still rejecting His Son today and sinning continually.

Mankind is polluting and destroying Gods' creation on our earth today so He will punish and judge mankind for their sins once and for all time and He will create a New Earth for the righteous men and women that He finds living on this present earth and give them the opportunity to live on His New created Earth where no sin will ever be found.

God said in Genesis 6:

[6] *And it repented the LORD that he had made man on the earth, and it grieved him at his heart.*

[7] *And the LORD said, I will destroy man whom I have created from the face of the earth; both man, and beast, and the creeping thing, and the fowls of the air; for it repenteth me that I have made them.*

God had searched all over this present earth during Noah's time and found only one righteous family and that was Noah's family which consisted of Noah, his wife and their three sons and their wives a total of eight people.

We need to search our lives continually and pray the following prayers found in:

Psalms Chapter 139: [3] *Search me, O God, and know my heart: try me, and know my thoughts:*

Psalms Chapter 51:[10] *Create in me a clean heart, O God; and renew a right spirit within me.*

Soon God instructed Noah to build a large boat constructed from gopher wood and to pitch it within and without with pitch and to call it the Ark. Pitch is a substance that comes in the form of liquid asphalt and was used as a waterproofing material.

Noah began gathering gopher wood and pitch from the surrounding area and told the local people that the materials was for the building of a boat that would float on water because it was going to rain so much that this present earth would be completely flooded by water. Noah warned the people of Gods' judgment but the people joked, laughed and made fun of him and his family. They began to ask each other, what is rain that this old man continues to talk about?

No one on our present earth had ever seen such a structure like this and had never even heard of a boat or rain. What in the world is this old man talking about.

As the people living on our present earth came to see Noah's progress in the building of this boat, Noah and his family soon became the talk and jokes of all their neighbors and all the people in the surrounding areas and towns.

During Noah's time the earth's surface was watered by a mist from below ground.

People on earth during Noah's time had never seen it rain and could not comprehend what he was even talking about. How could water fall from the sky, who ever heard of such a thing?

That old man must be crazy. Some say the old man has lost his marbles. Some think he is nuts. Many think he's been drinking some very strong wine and it has affected his mind. Many think his grape's has fermented.

Noah had been drinking but he had been drinking new wine from the wells of living water springing up from the Spirit of God, not a manmade drink that would have make him drunk.

Ladies and gentlemen we can still drink from this living water called Gods' Holy Spirit working in us thru the Holy Ghost the third entity of the Godhead. Seek God for His guidance by the Holy Ghost and receive His blessings. You will not be disappointed.

In Genesis 7: [1] *Noah received instructions from God to bring his family consisting of himself, his wife and their three sons and their wives, total of eight on board the Ark when it was finished because God had seen the righteousness of Noah during his generation.*

God also told Noah to load onto the Ark the following animals that God would send to the Ark. Seven pair each of clean beast, seven pair each of fowls of the air and two pairs each of unclean beast and food for all.

What a sight it must have been for the people on our present earth to witness. All at once there were animals coming from everywhere, down the main streets of their towns and cities, across their lawns, down their roads, thru the trees and fields all heading toward the Ark of Noah's that he called a boat.

I can just hear Noah's neighbors conversing with each other. Did you see all those animals when they came by? Wonder where they came from? I've lived in this country all my life and I have never seen or heard of some of those animals. Some people have said that they were going toward the structure that old crazy man Noah has been building out of gopher wood that he calls an Ark. Come on let's go see.

He must have some kind of magical powers to get all those animals to respond to him like that, my kids don't even respond to me that way.

Soon after the last animal came on board and the door was shut, guess what, seven days later water started falling from the sky and water spouts are shooting up from the earth's surface below.

What a site for the people on this present earth. People were dancing, running and splashing around in the water for a while but soon people began to realize that the water was getting deeper and deeper. No longer were they dancing, running, splashing and having fun in the water anymore. Panic and chaos began to set in. Water was starting to cover the ground.

Genesis 7: 4 states that it rained upon the earth for forty days and forty nights.

The Ark was starting to float up from the surface of the earth just as Noah had said.

Very soon someone commented, maybe that old man Noah was not so crazy after all and they all started running toward the Ark. They started pounding on the door and sides of the Ark panicking, asking and screaming to be let in but the door was shut tight.

The Word of God tells us that God had shut the door and now it was too late for those on the outside to get on board. Only Noah and his family a total of eight people were safe on board and soon they would be the only people left alive on our present earth along with the animals that God had sent to come on board the Ark.

Per bible history Noah was approximately six hundred years old when God caused the earth to flood.

Soon God will shut the door for mankind to receive the gift of salvation by grace provided by Jesus who shed His blood on the cross for the forgiveness of sins for people on our present earth. It will be too late for a lot of people to experience salvation just as it was during Noah's time.

Please accept Jesus as you Savior today and ask forgiveness for your sins before it's too late.

It states in **Verse Twenty Four of Chapter Seven of Genesis** that the waters prevailed upon this present earth for one hundred and fifty days. Noah, his family and all the animals stayed in the ark for fifty four more days for a total of two hundred and four days living in the Ark. After two hundred and four days living in the Ark, the Bible states that the water on our present earth had receded and the earth was dry enough to sustain life again.

Everything on this present earth had been destroyed, all mankind, all animals and all plant life except those in the Ark.

God remembered Noah and his family and all the animals on board the Ark and scripture states that God instructed Noah to leave the ark and God blessed Noah and his family and instructed them to be fruitful, multiply and replenish our present earth.

God made a covenant with Noah as seen in the following scriptures.

Genesis Chapter 9:

[**11**] *And I will establish my covenant with you; neither shall all flesh be cut off any more by the waters of a flood; neither shall there anymore be a flood to destroy the earth.*

[**12**] *And God said, This is the token of the covenant which I make between me and you and every living creature that is with you, for perpetual generations:*

[**13**] *I do set my bow in the cloud, and it shall be for a token of a covenant between me and the earth.*

[**14**] *And it shall come to pass, when I bring a cloud over the earth, that the bow shall be seen in the cloud:*

[**15**] *And I will remember my covenant, which is between me and you and every living creature of all flesh; and the waters shall no more become a flood to destroy all flesh.*

[**16**] *And the bow shall be in the cloud; and I will look upon it, that I may remember the everlasting covenant between God and every living creature of all flesh that is upon the earth.*

[**17**] *And God said unto Noah, This is the token of the covenant, which I have established between me and all flesh that is upon the earth.*

In verses eleven and twelve God states that He would never totally destroy this present earth again by a flood and as a token He would put a rainbow in the sky.

Pastor Ray Mills of the Praise and Worship Church in Broken Arrow, Oklahoma taught that during the flood the bow of the rainbow was pointed toward the ground with the ends pointing up toward God thus showing Gods' judgment being poured out on our present earth and mankind. Mankind may not have been able to see this rainbow but I believe it was there during this time.

After the flood God reversed the bow of the rainbow which is now pointing up toward God in Heaven with the ends pointing toward mankind on our present earth to remind God of the covenant He made with Noah not to ever destroy mankind or this present earth again with a flood.

Noah lived to the grand old age of Nine Hundred Fifty years. Noah and his wife had been blessed with three sons by the names of Japheth, Ham and Shem.

Japheth is commonly believed to be the father of the Europeans nations. The following scripture is a reference between Japheth and the Europeans nations: Genesis 10:5, which states: *"By these were the isles of the Gentiles divided in their lands."*

Ham, Noah's son had four sons Cush, Mizraim, Phut and Canaan, who are interpreted as having populated Africa and adjoining parts of Asia. The Bible refers to Egypt as "the land of Ham" in Psalms 78:51; 105:23, 27; 106:22; 1Ch 4:40.

Ham was the grandfather of Nimrod whose name means "Let us Revolt." We discussed this man earlier in this book.

Nimrod lived in the city of Babel in the land of Shinar which was in the region of Babylon. Nimrod decided to construct a tower that could reach into Heaven and he wanted to install a statue of his god Baal on top of this tower to be on equal basis with the true God.

This got Gods' attention very quickly so God came down to our present earth Himself to see this structure and decided the He could not allow this to happen so God confused man's language in such a way that they could not understand each other to continue their work.

It caused such mass confusion that work on this tower stopped and it was never finished.

This account in scripture is found in:

Genesis 11:

[1] *And the whole earth was of one language, and of one speech.*

[2] *And it came to pass, as they journeyed from the east, that they found a plain in* the *land of Shinar; and they dwelt there.*

This is talking about Nimrod a descendant of Ham the son of Noah.

[3] *And they said one to another, Go to, let us make brick, and burn them throughly. And they had brick for stone, and slime had they for morter.*

[4] *And they said, Go to, let us build us a city and a tower, whose top may reach unto heaven; and let us make us a name, lest we be scattered abroad upon the face of the whole earth.*

In this verse it shows that these people had a very ambition spirit not associated with God, they just wanted to make a name for themselves in direct rebellion to God.

Isn't this what a lot of people are doing today? Many are filled with pride and ambition endeavoring to make a name for themselves instead of giving the glory and honor to God for their accomplishments?

I have never seen a time since I become a Christian that it seems that everyone wants to be called an apostle or a prophet. Do you think the spirit of pride and ambition has crept into our churches, I think so?

Jesus commands us in the following verse to not even call anyone on earth our father:

Matthew 23 [9] *And call no man your father upon the earth: for one is your Father, which is in heaven.*

Back to Genesis Chapter 11:

[5] *And the LORD came down to see the city and the tower, which the children of men builded.*

[6] *And the LORD said, Behold, the people is one, and they have all one language; and this they begin to do: and now nothing will be restrained from them, which they have imagined to do.*

[7] *Go to, let us* ***(The Trinity Godhead)*** *go down, and there confound their language, that they may not understand one another's speech.*

[8] *So the LORD scattered them abroad from thence upon the face of all the earth: and they left off to build the city.*

[9] *Therefore is the name of it called Babel; because the LORD did there confound the language of all the earth: and from thence did the LORD scatter them abroad upon the face of all the earth.*

This was the second time that Lucifer has tried to become equal with God in Heaven.

Remember the first time was when he and the fallen angels rebelled against God in Genesis Chapter One Verse Two trying to locate his throne above God, and now this second time he used his influence thru Nimrod and the people of Babel in the land of Shinar who were trying to build this tower into heaven wanting to install his god Baal on top.

Shem became the father of the Nation of Ur or Elam or Persia which in today's modern world is called the Nation of Iran.

All the people of the world since the flood are descendants from the three sons of Noah. By these three sons of Noah were the nations on earth divided and replenished.

It says in Acts Chapter 17, Paul speaking about God:

[26] *And hath made of one blood all nations of men for to dwell on all the face of the earth, and hath determined the times before appointed, and the bounds of their habitation;*

[27] *That they should seek the Lord, if haply they might feel after him, and find him, though he be not far from every one of us:*

[28] *For in him we live, and move, and have our being; as certain also of your own poets have said, For we are also his offspring.*

[29] *Forasmuch then as we are the offspring of God, we ought not to think that the Godhead is like unto gold, or silver, or stone, graven by art and man's device.*

[30] *And the times of this ignorance God winked at; but now commandeth all men everywhere to repent:*

[31] *Because he hath appointed a day, in the which he will judge the world in righteousness by that man whom he hath ordained; whereof he hath given assurance unto all men, in that he hath raised him from the dead.*

As we continue our story concerning the history of our present earth we read of another great man by the name of Abram who was a descendent of Noah's son Shem. Abram's nationally was a Gentile not a Jew. Abram lived a total of one hundred seventy five years on our present earth.

One day God decided to pay a visit to Abram's home.

I wonder what we would do and say to God if He came to our home for a personal visit. Would He find a Bible on the table by our favorite chair or would it be stuck in a book shelf along with many other books covered in dust? What kind of a program would He find us watching on our televisions? Would He hear us using some not so religionist words some Christians use when they get excited, mad or upset?

I have heard some Christians speak some not so religionist words in their everyday conversations and even in God's House. God says that we will give an account for every idle word we speak.

Would God find believers acting, living and talking like the non-believers in our worldly society today when sometimes you really can't tell the believers from the unbelievers by the way some act, dress, live and talk?

If you are guilty of some of these things discussed here don't you think you are showing total disrespect for God or His house?

Remember what Jesus said and did to the money changers and their tables in the Temple and those who were selling merchandise to be used for sacrifices in the Temple. Jesus called them a den of thieves.

I'm sure they could have made the excuse or argument that they thought they were doing God and mankind a favor or a convenient service because they were making it convenient for the worshipers by providing them animals to buy to be used as a sacrifice to God but Jesus did not accept this excuse and He will not accept mine or your weak excuses either.

Do you think God is pleased with Christian's weak excuses for staying home from attending scheduled worship services in our churches or for pastors who cancel the evening service in our churches on our dedicated Sabbath using weak excuses?

One Pentecostal pastor told me that Sunday which is the dedicated Sabbath for most Christian Churches that in his church they did not have worship services on Sunday evening because they observed Sunday evening as family night. I asked him why they could not have family night on Friday or Saturday evening and he just became silent and did not have an answer for me.

Ladies and gentlemen we need to get serious about serving God. God is coming for a Bride that is without spot or wrinkle. He will not accept a blemished bride for His Son Jesus. That is a fact per scripture not just my statement.

A lot of our churches are becoming more like social places which promotes secular events taking the place of their worship services. Our churches should be promoting the House of God as a place of worship for worshiping God not a social place for men and women to gather for their worldly enjoyment. Many churches now have areas in their foyer that serve all kinds of drinks and food to eat in their auditorium during the worship service. How can we worship God during our worship services while we are drinking coffee, pop or tea and eating candy and food during our worship services? I realize that if you have a medical problem and need water to drink that is ok but most of the time it is just a habit. Just food for thought I am not judging anyone, that's Gods' job as seen in the following scriptures:

Matthew 21:

[12] *And Jesus went into the temple of God, and cast out all them that sold and bought in the temple, and overthrew the tables of the moneychangers, and the seats of them that sold doves,*

[13] *And said unto them, It is written, My house shall be called the house of prayer; but ye have made it a den of thieves.*

During this visit with Abram, God instructed him to pack up all his earthly processions, his wife Sarai and Lot his brother Haran's son, his servants and instructed him to leave his homeland and journey to a land toward the south that God would lead him to. God told Abram that He would make him the father of many nations and would bless him and make his name great. Abram was approximately seventy five years old when he received this visit from God.

Abram fully trusted God so much that he journeyed without question southward thru Canaan to a mountain range on the east side of Bethel. He then continued his journey south into Egypt because of the famine in the land, than he left Egypt and traveled back to Bethel where he had first camped during the beginning of his journey.

A lot of events happened to Abram along this journey which we do not have room to write about in this book. I recommend you read about the journeys and life of Abram in the book of Genesis, they are very interesting.

One thing I truly believe is that Abram loved and trusted God and God loved Abram as seen in the following scripture and he was called the Friend of God. WOW!

James 2: [23] *And the scripture was fulfilled which saith,* ***Abraham*** *believed God, and it was imputed unto him for righteousness: and he was called the Friend of God.*

One of Abram's kinsmen that journeyed with him was his brother Haran's son by the name of Lot. During this journey both Abram and Lot were blessed mightily by God and both became very rich with goods, cattle and other animals.

They had increased so much through the blessings from God that their herdsmen began striving with each other for food and water for their herds and having trouble keeping their herds of animals separated so Abram and Lot decided it would be best if they split up.

Abram being such a loving generous uncle told Lot to pick any direction that he wanted to go and he Abram would go the other way. Abram followed God by faith and not by sight while his nephew Lot chose his way of life by sight and not by faith in God.

The human side of Lot saw the lush green valleys of Jordan with plenty of water and food for his herds and journeyed in the direction of the cities of Sodom and Gomorrah. The below scripture ten states that these valleys of Jordan were similar to the Garden of the Lord (Eden). Later Lot moved his family into these cities as seen in the following scriptures.

Genesis 13:

[10] *And* **Lot** *lifted up his eyes, and beheld all the plain of Jordan, that it was well watered everywhere, before the LORD destroyed Sodom and Gomorrah, even as the garden of the LORD, like the land of Egypt, as thou comest unto Zoar.*

[11] *Then* **Lot** *chose him all the plain of Jordan; and* **Lot** *journeyed east: and they separated themselves the one from the other.*

[12] *Abram dwelled in the land of Canaan, and* **Lot** *dwelled in the cities of the plain, and pitched his tent toward Sodom.*

Sometimes in our journey thru life we take the easy way but it is not always the right way as Lot later found out.

For approximately four thousand years God dealt with mankind Himself on our present earth, sometimes using angels in His dealing with mankind just like God did with Lot as seen below.

On one such occasion God and two angels paid a visit to Abram. Scripture said that it was God who remained with Abram while the two other angels went to visit Lot in Sodom and Gomorrah. Sodom and Gomorrah were real cities located in the Jordan valley on our present earth.

The two angels had a hard time convincing Lot, his wife and two of his daughters into leaving these cities but after much persuading and giving instructions to them to not look back after leaving these cities because God was going to destroy these cities with fire and brimstone as judgment for being such sinful cities.

God did destroy these cities but only Lot and his two daughters were saved from this destruction because Lot's wife who started the journey with them disobeyed Gods' instructions given to Lot and his family by the two angels. Lots wife by turning and looking back toward these cities was turned into a pillar of salt per the following scripture.

Gen.19 : [26] *But his wife looked back from behind him, and she became a* ***pillar of salt****.*

Lot later became the father of the nations of Moab whose people were called Moabites with its location east of the Dead Sea and Ammon whose people were called Ammonites, whose dwelling-place was on the east of the Dead Sea and Jordan. These two nations were birthed thru his descendants by his two daughters who got him drunk and had sex with him thus becoming pregnant.

Ladies and gentlemen it does not pay to look back into sin after God has rescued you from sin by His salvation provided by the death of His Son Jesus on the cross as seen in the following scriptures.

Hebrews 6:

[4] *For it is impossible for those who were once enlightened* ***(saved),*** *and have* ***tasted*** *of the heavenly gift, and were made partakers of the Holy Ghost,*

[5] *And have* ***tasted*** *the good word of God, and the powers of the world to come,*

[6] *If they shall fall away, to renew them again unto repentance; seeing they crucify to themselves the Son of God afresh, and put him to an open shame.*

Many teach that once you have ask forgiveness for your sins that you will always be saved. I believe this teaching could deceive the people living on Our Present Earth and in our Churches who have accepted Jesus as their Savior into thinking they can live any way they want to and still be saved and still be rewarded by eternal life. Such teaching as this could cause a lot of people to miss the Catching up of the Church and be doomed to receive eternal life in hell with Satan.

I believe the above scriptures are speaking about those who were once enlightened (saved) if they should fall away to renew them again unto repentance, this means that it is almost impossible, but the God I serve is very merciful and forgiving.

The only un-forgiving sin is the blasphemy of the Holy Ghost.

I wonder what God thinks about the sinful leadership of some of our cities and nations on our present earth including the United States. Some nations including the United States are condoning the same sinful sins that was prevalent in Sodom and Gomorrah before they were destroyed by God.

God will pass judgment on our nation and the sins of mankind if we don't change and ask Him for forgiveness and began to worship Him and His Son Jesus in spirit and in truth as seen in the following scriptures.

John 4:

[23] *But the hour cometh, and now is, when the true worshippers shall worship the Father in* ***spirit and in truth****: for the Father seeketh such to worship him.*

[24] *God is a Spirit: and they that worship him must worship him in* ***spirit and in truth****.*

Abram was married to a beautiful lady by the name of Sarai. Abram and Sarai was very excited about the previous visit from God informing Abraham that he would become the father of many nations but wondered how this was going to come to pass since Sarai and Abram had no children. Sarai was barren and now both were getting very old and still no children born to them.

During the time of Abram on our present earth if the wife was barren it was a reproach to her as a woman and other women looked down on the barren wife. I am sure there was a lot of gossip in the camp between the other women concerning Sarai being barren so after a while Sarai started wondering if God was correct or if God had forgotten the promise He made her husband Abram about becoming the father of many nations.

Sarai was getting more anxious and impatient every day and very concerned about not having a son to carry on the family name for Abram. Sarai was also aware that she was getting older everyday so she decided it was time to help God out just in case He had forgotten His promise made to Abram about becoming the father of many nations.

Have you ever prayed for an answer to a problem and then got impatient and tried to fix what you prayed for in life yourself instead of waiting for God to fix it? I have and most of the time it creates problems doesn't it?

Abram while journeying into Egypt had purchased Sarai a beautiful young Egyptian handmaid servant by the name of Hagar during this journey. Sarai decided to give Hagar to Abram who is now the age of eighty six for his second wife and maybe they would have a son to help God out concerning His promise to Abram in becoming the father of many nations. Since she legally owned Hagar as a servant, any children born to Hagar would be considered Sarah's children, problem solved or maybe not.

Why does mankind always think God needs help and tries to help God out?

I think God can handle any situation that mankind experiences on our present earth don't you? In the follow scripture it states that nothing is impossible with God.

Luke 1: [37] *For with God nothing shall be impossible.*

This was trouble from the very start. Guess what, Hagar soon conceived and was with child and soon a baby boy was born and they named him Ishmael.

Abram was approximately eighty six years old when Ishmael was born.

For a while everyone was happy, new baby in the home, watching him learning to walk and talk. Soon the glamor of everyday life with the new baby wore off and Sarai realized Ishmael was not her son even though Sarai legally owned Hagar who was her handmaid servant and could claim Ishmael as her son.

Ladies and gentlemen this was not Gods' plan concerning Abram becoming the father of many nations. This was man's plan and trouble and strife soon began in the home between Sarai and Hagar.

I think most of you wives would agree that this arrangement would not work with you in your marriage. I know it would not work with my wife in our marriage.

Sarai soon became very jealous of Hagar and Ishmael and their relationship with Abram. In retaliation Hagar began making derogatory remarks about Sarai being barren and reminded Sarai that she Hagar had given Abram a son to carry on the family name not Sarai. Sarai was becoming more and more agitated every day and soon became very cruel, mean and hateful to Hagar. I am sure she was giving Abram a hard time also reminding him that she was the first wife and had taken care of him for a long time.

Sadly to say, some Christians become very cruel, mean and hateful if they don't get their way. It's their way or no way. Let's look at the following scripture found in **Proverbs 16: Verse 32** *He that is slow to anger is better than the mighty; and he that ruleth his spirit than he that taketh a city.*

Don't allow yourself to become this type of Christian who is so self-centered that you cannot accept that you might be in the wrong. We need to seek God for His guidance thru the Holy Ghost in our lives.

Abram was at his wits end, no peace in the home anymore. Two beautiful women in his life fighting each other, what was he going to do? He was trying to please both but he was still in love with Sarai his first love even though he had acquired special feelings for Hagar also. After some research I find that the Egyptian women were very much like today's women they used a lot of make-up around the eyes and face with some kind of metal jewelry. They usually wore their hair which was a dark shade in braids or something like a pony tail so Hagar probably was a very young beautiful lady.

At the age of ninety nine God gave Abram the sign of the covenant of circumcision as a token of the covenant between God and Abraham and his seed after him. He was to circumcise all males in his family both family and servants, which he did.

Genesis Chapter Seventeen is when God changed Abram's name to Abraham and Sarai name to Sarah.

Soon Abraham at the age of one hundred years old became a father again and a son was born to him and Sarah and Isaac was circumcised on the eight day per God's instructions in His covenant with Abraham.

God does not and will not change His plans for our lives. God will not forget His promises made to us. God did not forget His promise made to Abraham.

This little guy's name was Isaac and it was thru him not Ishmael that the covenant of the promise seed Jesus would be born.

Finally Abraham had enough of this constant fighting between Sarah and Hagar so he told Sarah to do as she pleased with Hagar and her son Ishmael even though Abraham loved his son Ishmael. Soon Sarah instructed Hagar that she and Ishmael would have to leave and instructed her to never come back. Problem solved, only time will tell.

In the following scriptures we now see Hagar and Ishmael wandering in the desert sitting under a bush about to die from the heat, thirsty and starving, no food or water. Oh but God had not forgotten them. Scripture says that the angel of God called out to Hagar and got her attention then God opened her eyes and showed Hagar a well of water and instructed Hagar to draw and give drink to the child.

God says in His Word to pray for those who despitefully use us and if we will listen to God and be led by the Holy Ghost we will reap the blessing of God just as Hagar and Ishmael did as seen in the following scriptures.

Genesis 21:

[10] *Wherefore she* ***(Sarah)*** *said unto Abraham, Cast out this bondwoman* ***(Hagar)*** *and her son* ***(Ishmael)****: for the son of this bondwoman shall not be heir with my son, even with Isaac.*

[11] *And the thing was very grievous in Abraham's sight because of his son.*

[12] *And God said unto Abraham, Let it not be grievous in thy sight because of the lad, and because of thy bondwoman; in all that Sarah hath said unto thee, hearken unto her voice; for in Isaac shall thy seed be called.*

[13] *And also of the son of the bondwoman will I make a nation, because he is thy seed.*

[14] *And Abraham rose up early in the morning, and took bread, and a bottle of water, and gave it unto Hagar, putting it on her shoulder, and the child, and sent her away: and she departed, and wandered in the wilderness of Beer-sheba.*

[15] *And the water was spent in the bottle, and she cast the child under one of the shrubs.*

[16] *And she went, and sat her down over against him a good way off, as it were a bowshot: for she said, Let me not see the death of the child. And she sat over against him, and lift up her voice, and wept.*

[17] *And God heard the voice of the lad; and the angel of God called Hagar out of heaven, and said unto her, What aileth thee, Hagar? fear not; for God hath heard the voice of the lad where he is.*

[18] *Arise, lift up the lad, and hold him in thine hand; for I will make him a great nation.*

[19] *And God opened her eyes, and she saw a well of water; and she went, and filled the bottle with water, and gave the lad drink.*

Hagar did reap the blessing of God because the following scripture states that God made twelve princes from the loins of her son Ishmael and made him a great nation as seen in verse twenty below because of Gods' friend Abraham.

Genesis 17: [20] *And as for Ishmael, I have heard thee: Behold, I have blessed him, and will make him fruitful, and will multiply him exceedingly; twelve princes shall he beget, and I will make him a great nation.*

The twelve princes were Nebajoth, Kedar, Adbeel, Mibsam, Mishma, Dumah, Massa, Hadar, Tema, Jetur, Naphish and Kedemah who were the fathers of many of our Middle Eastern Muslim Nations today.

The angel of the Lord also told Hagar that God had heard and seen her affliction but that Ishmael would be a wild man and his hand will be against every man, and every man's hand would be against him. This scripture is still being fulfilled on our present earth today thru wars and religionist persecution's even as I am writing this book.

God did not and will not condone the sin of disobedience but due to the obedience and faithfulness and prayers of Abraham to God, God blessed all the descendants of Abraham.

God does not and will not change His plans for our lives. God does not forget His promises made to us. God did not forget His promise made to Abraham.

In **Chapter 22 of Genesis** the following verses confirms the Abrahamic covenant that God made with Abraham.

In this Chapter we find God asking Abraham to offer his son Isaac as a sacrifice and Abraham laying Isaac on an alter to offer him as a sacrifice to God but God seeing that Abraham remained faithful in his service to God intervened and provided a ram caught in a bush to offer as the sacrifice instead of Isaac. Abraham passed Gods' test.

[15] *And the angel of the LORD called unto Abraham out of heaven the second time,*

[16] *And said, By myself have I sworn, saith the LORD, for because thou hast done this thing, and hast not withheld thy son, thine only son:*

[17] *That in blessing I will bless thee, and in multiplying I will multiply thy seed as the stars of the heaven, and as the sand which is upon the sea shore; and thy seed shall possess the gate of his enemies;*

[18] *And in thy seed shall all the nations of the earth be blessed; because thou hast obeyed my voice.*

After twenty eight years enjoying her son Isaac, Sarah died at the age of one hundred twenty seven years.

Thirteen years later after the death of Sarah, Abraham at the age of one hundred and forty years old married another woman by the name of Keturah and they had six sons Zimran, Jokshan, Medan, Midian, Ishbak and Shuah. These six sons of Abraham fathered many nations that make up the Arabic Nations on our present earth today.

God blessed Abraham all the days of his life and he did become the father of many nations which consist of The Nation of Israel, the Islamic Nations and the Arabic Nations just as God promised, why, because he was faithful to God and it was accounted unto him for righteousness.

Galatians 3:

[6] *Even as Abraham believed God, and it was accounted to him for righteousness.*

[7] *Know ye therefore that they which are of faith, the same are the children of Abraham.*

[8] *And the scripture, foreseeing that God would justify the heathen through faith, preached before the gospel unto Abraham, saying, In thee shall all nations be blessed.*

[9] *So then they which be of faith are blessed with faithful Abraham.*

If we believe that we are saved by faith, then we are also the children of Abraham per verse seven above.

Many Christians wonder why God blesses some Christians and does not bless them. Maybe God as He looks at your life does not find you being very faithful to Him. We need to search our lives daily and make sure we are found being faithful to God just like Abraham. If we are faithful, scripture says that God will pour out blessings on us that we can't contain.

Ladies and gentlemen just remember that the Israelis, Muslim and Arabic people are all related to each other thru the blood line of their father Abraham. The problem is that they all believe they are the promised people. But scripture states that the promise seed **(singular not plural)** would came from the blood line of Isaac the son of Abraham and Sarah thru their grandson Jacob who was Isaac and Rebekah's youngest son not thru the sons of the other wives of Abraham.

Our journey thru the Bible on our present earth reveals a lot of special people that God chose and used to do His will. It would take a very big book to name them all but let's just look at a few more of these:

Abraham's son Isaac lived one hundred eighty years. Isaac was forty years old when he married Rebekah and was the father of Esau and Jacob. Esau being the eldest son should have received the family's birthright blessing and his father Isaac's blessing but due to his bad attitude God gave the birthright blessing to Jacob the youngest son.

Esau a hunter coming home one day from a hunting trip being very hungry sold his birthright to Jacob for some bread and pottage of lentils. The birthright blessing gave the one receiving this blessing the inheritance to his father's estate along with the leadership and responsibility over all his family.

Hunger will make people do things that they would not normally do. During the end time seven year tribulation period Satan working thru the antichrist will require everyone to receive a mark or number to be able to buy or sell.

Hunger will entice a lot of people maybe even some Christians to take and receive Satan's mark called the Mark of the Beast to survive. There is no redemption for mankind who takes Satan's Mark of the Beast as seen in the following scriptures.

Revelation 14:

[9] *And the third angel followed them, saying with a loud voice, If any man worship the beast and his image, and receive his mark in his forehead, or in his hand,*

[10] *The same shall drink of the wine of the wrath of God, which is poured out without mixture into the cup of his indignation; and he shall be tormented with fire and brimstone in the presence of the holy angels, and in the presence of the Lamb:*

[11] *And the smoke of their torment ascendeth up for ever and ever: and they have no rest day nor night, who worship the beast and his image, and whosoever receiveth the mark of his name.*

Esau being very upset decided to kill his brother Jacob after Jacob following the instructions of his mother Rebekah deceived his father Isaac into believing he was Esau and received the blessing of his father Isaac instead of Esau. Now Jacob had Esau's birthright blessing and also the blessing of their father Isaac. The birthright blessing and the father's blessing was supposed to go to the eldest son but in this case Esau as the eldest had such a bad attitude that God in His infinite wisdom gave these blessings to Jacob the youngest.

God cannot and will not use people with bad attitudes. We should all, this includes me pray the following prayers found in the following scriptures.

Psalms 139 Verse [23] *Search me, O God, and know my heart: try me, and know my thoughts:*

Psalms 51 Verse [10] *Create in me a clean heart, O God; and renew a right spirit within me.*

Esau in rebellion to his parents married two women of the Hittites of the Nation of Canaan, which scripture said were a grief to Isaac and Rebekah.

This was against Gods' instructions. They were to marry within their own family blood line.

Than Esau with his bad attitude rebelled again and married one of the daughters of Ishmael his grandfather Abraham's son conceived thru Hagar, Sarah's Egyptian handmaid. He not only rebelled against his parent's wishes but this was a direct rebellion against Gods' instructions concerning marriage.

Esau is the father of the nation of Edom or the Edomite people. This country today is a province located in southwestern Jordan.

Jacob being informed by his mother that Esau planned to kill him fled to the country of Haran to the home of Laban who was the brother of his mother Rebekah and while there married two wives, Leah and Rachel who were sisters and the daughters of Laban.

Jacob had twelves sons, Reuben, Simeon, Levi, Judah, Issachar, Zebulun, Benjamin, Dan, Naphtali, Gad, Asher and Joseph between these two wives Leah and Rachel and their maids Bilhah and Zilpah.

Jacob had served Laban for seven years and thought he was receiving Rebekah who was the youngest daughter for his wife for his services but Laban giving him a bachelor party the night of the wedding getting him drunk and gave him Leah the eldest daughter instead of Rebekah for his wife. Jacob loved Rebekah so much that he agreed to serve Laban another seven years so that he could marry Rebekah also.

These twelve sons of Jacob became the fathers of the twelve tribes of Israel but only Judah who was the son of Leah is the true father of the Jews.

Joseph the youngest son of Jacob at that time was sold by his brother's to a group of merchants traveling to Egypt because of their jealous spirit. Due to Joseph's faith in God he later became the second ruler in Egypt second only to the Pharaoh and during the time of seven years of famine saved his entire family and the Nation of Egypt from starvation. A lot of people believe that Christians should stay out of politics but look at the life of Joseph, as stated above he became the second ruler in Egypt answering only to the Pharaoh. This was Gods' plan for the creation of the Nation of Israel.

We need Christian politicians in our government.

God later changed Jacob's name to Israel and then God named a nation that he had chosen from among all the nations on earth to be His own and called that nation Israel which was made up from the twelve sons from the loins of Jacob.

Pastor Ray Mills, senior pastor of Praise and Worship Church in Broken Arrow, Oklahoma made a very profound statement during his Sunday Morning message that Israel is the only Nation on our present earth that was named by God all other nations were named by man.

Next in our story we come to a man by the name of Moses whose mother was a daughter of Levi. Moses' father Amram was a descendent of Levi one of the twelve sons of Jacob. Moses was born to this Israeli family while they were living in bondage to the Egyptians in Egypt.

Due to the increasing population growth of the Hebrew people of the Nation of Israel, Egypt's king called Pharaoh had instructed the Hebrew midwives that all the Hebrew baby boys were to be killed. Pharaoh was trying to stop the growth of this Hebrew nation but the girl babies could be kept alive.

The Hebrew midwives refused to do this because it was against the teaching of God so Pharaoh gave the order for his soldiers to search the homes of all the Hebrew family's and to kill all the boy babies.

If Satan thru Pharaoh had been successful in killing all the Israeli boy babies he would have stopped the promise seed Jesus from being born.

The mother of Moses hid him for three months in the rushes and flags growing along the banks of the Nile River in a little waterproof basket determined to save his life. Moses' sister Miriam would go down to the river every day to watch him to make sure he was safe.

One day during the hot summer months, one of the hottest day of the year, Pharaoh' daughter was swimming and bathing in the Nile River when she hears the cries of a baby. She along with her handmaids searched along the bank of the Nile River looking thru the rushes and finds a little basket with a baby Hebrew boy inside. Pharaoh's daughter loved him instantly. Miriam, Moses' sister seeing Pharaoh's daughter find Moses and being close by ask her if she needed a nanny for this child and when she said yes, guess who Miriam recommended, Moses' own mother of course. So Moses' mother got to be his nanny and raised him for Pharaoh' daughter, God in action.

During this encounter they named him Moses and Pharaoh' daughter raised him to be her own son with the help of Moses' own mother.

Later after Moses being a young man at the age of forty years being schooled in all the ways of the Egyptians in Egypt was watching the Hebrew slaves making bricks when he saw one of the Egyptians taskmasters beating a Hebrew slave. Moses intervened and during this fight Moses slew and buried the dead Egyptian taskmaster.

Some of the Hebrew slaves saw Moses kill and bury the Egyptian. Moses thinking they would tell the other Egyptians that he had killed the taskmaster fled the country of Egypt due to fear of reprisal from the Pharaoh who knew the true background of Moses that he was a Hebrew not an Egyptian even though the Pharaoh's daughter called Moses her son.

Later we find Moses after he fled Egypt living on the back side of the desert doing the duties of a shepherd when he saw a bush on fire but it was not burning up.

God used this burning bush to get Moses' attention and when he stopped to investigate why the bush was not being burned up God instructed Moses to remove his shoes because the ground he was standing on was Holy Ground.

God instructed Moses to return back to Egypt and to tell the Pharaoh who was not the same Pharaoh that Moses knew when he was growing up in Egypt to release Gods' people so they could travel from Egypt to a land of their own. God told Moses that all who had been seeking his life for killing the Egyptian taskmaster had died.

The Pharaoh of Egypt who was considered a god by the Egyptians was very reluctant to let the Hebrew people leave Egypt because they were his slaves. God thru Moses told the Pharaoh that God would send plagues on the land of Egypt and the Egyptian people if he did not let the Hebrew people leave Egypt.

Pharaoh who thought he was a god would not recognize God as the True God of the Nation of Israel but finally after many plagues and the deaths of all first born males of the Nation of Egypt the Pharaoh finally gave permission for the Hebrew people to leave.

It was Moses along with his brother Aaron whom God chose as leaders to lead Gods' people out of bondage in Egypt toward the promise land that God had promised Abraham.

After the Hebrew people left Egypt the Pharaoh soon decided that he had made a big mistake and along with his army tried to overtake the Hebrews at the shore of the Red Sea but the Bible states that God pronounced judgment on Pharaoh and his armies and all were drown in the Red Sea. God had parted the waters of the Red Sea so that the Hebrew people could walk over on dry land and then released the waters upon the Pharaoh and his Egyptian armies drowning them all as they followed the Hebrew people across the Red Sea.

Just before leaving Egypt, God gave Moses instructions for all the Hebrew people to ask for and to borrow from the Egyptians golden jewels, silver jewels and other expensive items and scripture states that God gave the Hebrew people favor in the sight of the Egyptians.

Have you ever wondered why the Hebrew people needed all this silver, gold, brass and other materials? I have and one Saturday morning as I was studying Gods' word the following thoughts came into my mind, I call these golden nuggets from God.

God was giving the Hebrew people who were slaves while living in Egypt, the necessary materials that would be needed to build Gods' Tabernacle while they wandered in the wilderness. The Hebrew people did not have enough gold, silver, brass, fine linens or jewelry themselves while living in Egypt as slaves to build God His Tabernacle.

God used the wealth of Satan's people the Egyptians to fund the building of His Tabernacle in the wilderness. What a God we serve.

Proverbs 13: says in verse twenty two:

[22] A good man leaveth an inheritance to his children's children: and **the wealth** of the sinner is laid up for the just.

My King James Bible states that the Hebrew people brought so much gold, silver and other materials to the men building Gods' Tabernacle that those in charge requested to Moses that he tell the people to stop donating materials since those building the Tabernacle had an over-abundance of materials.

My King James Bible give reference to the dollar amount of gold, silver, precious stones, linen materials and brass and other materials that was used in the building of this Tabernacle.

I have listed some of the monetary values of these materials computed when my version of the King James Bible was written.

1. Gold, $5,569,284.00 dollars.
2. Silver, $ 1,062,248.00 dollars.
3. Brass, no dollar value given but they used 7,080 lbs.
4. Fine Linens, no value given.
5. Precious Stones, no value given.

Wow, what a sight for anyone living on our present earth to see when this tabernacle was finished. God gave knowledge and ability for all involved in the construction of His Tabernacle.

During our Christian walk on this present earth, God is training each and every one of us with the knowledge and ability to rule and reign with Jesus on the New Earth.

I get excited just thinking about Gods' Holy City with its street of Gold and foundations of precious jewels that will be located on the New Earth created by God. Just think you and I will get to enjoy the beauty this city for eternity, are you excited?

God gave special instructions and ordained special people from the Israeli tribes for the tearing down and setting up of the Tabernacle when they were journeying and the Tabernacle was to be set up only one time each year and that was on the first day of the first month of each year per the following scriptures.

Exodus 40:

[1] *And the LORD spake unto Moses, saying,*

[2] *On the first day of the first month shalt thou set up the tabernacle of the tent of the congregation.*

[17] *And it came to pass in the first month in the second year, on the first day of the month, that the tabernacle was reared up.*

[34] *Then a cloud covered the tent of the congregation, and the glory of the LORD filled the tabernacle.*

[35] *And Moses was not able to enter into the tent of the congregation, because the cloud abode thereon, and the glory of the LORD filled the tabernacle.*

[36] *And when the cloud was taken up from over the tabernacle, the children of Israel went onward in all their journeys:*

[37] *But if the cloud were not taken up, then they journeyed not till the day that it was taken up.*

[38] *For the cloud of the LORD was upon the tabernacle by day, and fire was on it by night, in the sight of all the house of Israel, throughout all their journeys.*

As long as the cloud of the Gods' glory was upon the tabernacle the children of Israel did not journey forward. When the cloud lifted the tabernacle was torn down and they journeyed forward.

We find in the book of Exodus God giving Moses instructions for the building of this Tabernacle, the Ark of the Covenant, the Mercy Seat, the Cherubim's, the Altars, the Curtains, the golden Candlesticks, the Anointing Oil, the Tub for washing the priest' hands and feet and all the other items needed for the sacrifices to God. We find that Gods' favorite colors are listed in the Book of Exodus. They are blue, purple, scarlet and red.

Wow, what a magnificent God we serve.

The Hebrews people who made up the Nation of Israel wandered in the wilderness eighty years under the leadership of Moses because of their grumbling and disobedience of God.

Many of you will think that I was mistaken in saying eighty years instead of forty years as most of us have been taught during our life time so we will discuss thus further while discussing another man by the name of Joshua below.

Moses as the leader of the Israeli people and Aaron as the Israeli Priest never got to enter into the promise land. Moses only got to come to the border of the promise land because he got so angry one day with the people of Israel for their grumbling against God that he disobeyed God who had told him to speak to a rock so that water would come out of it for the Israeli people to drink and to water their flocks.

In his frustration with the people of Israel Moses struck the rock twice instead of speaking to the rock as God had instructed him to do. Due to Moses and Aaron's disobedience to God they were not allowed to enter into the promise land. This account is found in **Numbers Chapter 20:**
[**24**] *Aaron shall be gathered unto his people: for he shall not enter into the land which I have given unto the children of Israel, because ye rebelled against my word at the water of Meribah.*

Aaron as the man God had chosen to be the priest to the Nation of Israel should have given Moses spiritual instructions to speak to the rock instead of striking the rock. He agreed with Moses instead of following the instructions of God.

Ladies and gentlemen we need to be very careful to do the work correctly that God has called us to do on this present earth. God may not find us qualified to do His work on the New Earth if we can't follow His instructions on our present earth.

Many men and women on our present earth who will not accept Jesus as their Savior will not get to enter the Kingdom of God which will be located on the New Earth because of their disobedience in not accepting Jesus as their Savior just as Moses and Aaron were not allowed to enter the promise land.

The Bible states that Moses died and God buried him in a valley in the land of Moab, over against Beth-peor: but no man knoweth of his sepulchre unto this day found in the scriptures below.

I believe God transported the spirit of Moses directly to Paradise located in the center of our present earth at that time but Paradise is now located in Heaven. Before his death God did take Moses upon a high mountain and allowed him to see into the promise land that He God had given to the Nation of Israel as seen in the following scriptures.

Deuteronomy 34:

[1] *And Moses went up from the plains of Moab unto the mountain of Nebo, to the top of Pisgah, that is over against Jericho. And the LORD shewed him all the land of Gilead, unto Dan,*

[2] *And all Naphtali, and the land of Ephraim, and Manasseh, and all the land of Judah, unto the utmost sea,*

[3] *And the south, and the plain of the valley of Jericho, the city of palm trees, unto Zoar.*

[4] *And the LORD said unto him, This is the land which I sware unto Abraham, unto Isaac, and unto Jacob, saying, I will give it unto thy seed: I have caused thee to see it with thine eyes, but thou shalt not go over thither.*

[5] *So Moses the servant of the LORD died there in the land of Moab, according to the word of the LORD.*

[6] *And he (God) buried him in a valley in the land of Moab, over against Beth-peor: but no man knoweth of his sepulchre unto this day.*

[7] *And Moses was an hundred and twenty years old when he died: his eye was not dim, nor his natural force abated.*

Many nations have tried and are still trying to take this land away from the Nation of Israel even as I am writing this book. This land was ordained by God and given to the Nation of Israel as an inheritance and no one will ever be successful in taking this land away from Israel.

Many presidents and government leaders have tried and are still trying to draft treaties between Israel and other Arab and Muslim nations with no success due to trying to persuade Israel to give up their land for peace. The man who will become the antichrist during the Seven Year Tribulation Period will draft a seven year treaty with the Nation of Israel promising peace and protection but will break this treaty agreement after three and one half years.

Many of the Israeli prime ministers who have agreed to give up some of Israel's land for peace have suffered death, sickness or have been removed from office.

God will not allow the land of Israel to be given away. This land of the Nation of Israel is Gods' property that God chose for Himself.

Next in our story we find a man by the name of Joshua of the tribe of Ephraim, called Oshea the son of Nun in Verse 8 of Numbers 14. Moses changed Oshea name to Jehoshua in Verse 16 pronounced Joshua who was the personal aide of Moses and the commanding general of the armies of Israel under the leadership of Moses.

Joshua was one of the twelve spies that Moses sent to spy out the promise land before the death of Moses.

Joshua was born at the beginning time that Israel left Egypt and had traveled all his life in the wilderness. Joshua was forty years old when Moses sent him along with eleven other men to spy out the promise land.

Joshua 14: [7] *Forty years old was I when Moses the servant of the LORD sent me from Kadesh-barnea to espy out the land; and I brought him word again as it was in mine heart.*

Joshua was eighty five years old when Moses died.

At the age of eighty five we find Joshua accepting leadership of the Nation of Israel and leading the people of Israel into the promise land after the death of Moses.

Joshua ruled over Israel for twenty five years and died at the age of one hundred ten years.

God parted the river of Jordan for Joshua just as He had done for Moses at the Red Sea so that the people of Israel could pass over on a dry river bed during flood stage. This crossing was by Jericho just before this city was destroyed by God.

God magnified Joshua on this day in the eyes of the people of Israel and scripture says that they feared or respected Joshua all the days of his life just like God magnified Moses in the eyes of the people.

Of the twelve men sent to spy out the promise land only Joshua and Caleb gave Moses a good report concerning Israel being able to occupy the promise land.

We need to be careful what we say and do because it may affect other people's lives like the bad report given by the ten spies affected all the Israeli people.

Israel had wandered in the wilderness for forty years before Moses sent these twelve men to spy out the promise land. The bad report given by the ten spies reporting to Moses caused the people of Israel to wander in the wilderness another forty years until all the males and men of war the age of twenty years and upward died in the wilderness as seen in the following scriptures.

Numbers 14:

[29] *Your carcases shall fall in this wilderness; and all that were numbered of you, according to your whole number, from twenty years old and upward, which have murmured against me,*

[32] *But as for you, your carcases, they shall fall in this wilderness.*

[33] *And your children shall wander in the wilderness forty years, and bear your whoredoms, until your carcases be wasted in the wilderness.*

[34] *After the number of the days in which ye searched the land, even forty days, each day for a year, shall ye bear your iniquities, even forty years, and ye shall know my breach of promise.*

[35] *I the LORD have said, I will surely do it unto all this evil congregation, that are gathered together against me: in this wilderness they shall be consumed, and there they shall die.*

This is a total of eighty years the children of Israel wandered in the wilderness.

We will have to give an account for our words that we speak as seen in the follow scripture.

Matthew 12: [36] *But I say unto you, That every idle word that men shall speak, they shall give account thereof in the day of judgment.*

After the death of Joshua, God used many different men to do his will in judging Israel but Gods' plan in the beginning was to use priest and judges to judge the Nation of Israel.

One such man was Jerubbaal who was also called Gideon in the book of Judges Chapter Seven defeating the Midianite armies with only three hundred men as he followed Gods' instructions using only lamps and trumpets.

Gideon started with a large army but God instructed him to send everyone home except three hundred men.

God knew that the people of Israel would think that they won this battle themselves thru their own strength if all the men stayed and fought. By only using three hundred men, all would know it was God who won the battle not the Israeli army.

After many different leaders in Israel we find a man by the name of Samson who was a prominent man that God used to fight the Philistines. Samson was a Nazarite unto the Lord and scripture states that as a Nazarite his hair was never to be cut and he was not to drink strong wine nor touch anything dead. We know Sampson broke two of the laws, He told Delilah about his strength being in his hair not being cut and it got cut off by the Philistines and he took honey from a dead lion and gave to his parents to eat, he had to touch this dead lion to get to the honey thus breaking the Nazarite vow.

Samson loved to visit the city of Gaza which was a sinful city full of prostitution and all manner of sexual sins. Samson was a true ladies man, big muscles, good looks with beautiful long hair and he enjoyed visiting this city and enjoyed the pleasures it provided him.

Ladies and gentlemen we may enjoy sin for a while, but the Bible states in **Numbers 32: [23]** *But if ye will not do so* ***(talking about repenting)****, behold, ye have sinned against the LORD: and be sure your sin will find you out.*

Samson had a weakness for women and this got him into a lot of trouble with man and God.

Delilah, one of his wayfaring women that he was attracted to was always trying to get Sampson to tell her the source of his strength. Finally one day Sampson confined to her that his strength was in his long hair which was never to be cut. She had tried numerous times to find out how Samson got his strength but he had never told her the truth before until this time.

After a long night of partying, Delilah was massaging Samson's head, rubbing his shoulders getting him relaxed and soon he was fast asleep with his head in Delilah's lap. Delilah signaled to the lords of the Philistines waiting close by who came up and paid her money for her services. Delilah than called for a barber who came in and cut off Samson's hair and lords of the Philistines bound Samson and in doing so Samson lost his supernatural strength as stated in Numbers 32:23 above be sure your sin will find you out.

Ladies and gentlemen if we play and sleep with the devil long enough he will find out our weakness and destroy our strength just like he did to Samson.

Scripture says that Delilah woke Samson up and said, Samson wake up the Philistines are here. Samson got up and shook himself as before but he did not have the strength of God in his body.

Sampson had played with the devil before and got away with it, but not this time, God said enough is enough just like He will soon say to mankind living on our present earth today.

Ladies and Gentlemen don't play with the devil. He will zap you of your strength in God just as he did with Samson.

The Philistines put Samson in prison. They put out his eyes, bound him with fetters of brass to the pole that turned the grinding wheel and used him to grind their grain. As he was turning the grinding wheel day after day his hair started to grow long again and he asked God to give him back his strength just one more time.

One day the lords of the Philistine gave a big feast and invited all the governors, all the royalty and many people to gather together in the coliseum with a beautiful blue sky above, the sun shining brightly not a cloud in the sky. The Philistines had gathered in the coliseum to offer Dagon their grain god a great sacrifice and soon began rejoicing and shouting great is our god who hath delivered Sampson our enemy into our hand which slew many of us and was the destroyer of our country. Soon their hearts became merry from much drinking and partying.

Samson hearing the sound of music and the games being played asked one of the young Philistine men guarding him what was going on. The young man told Samson about the sporting games and bragged about how many people were in attendance stating that the coliseum was filled to capacity with official leaders along with approximately three thousand men and women upon the roof top.

The Philistine leaders feeling very excited soon sent a young man for Samson so that they could make sport of him in front of all the people.

Samson informed the young man that he wanted to stand between the two large columns located on the ground floor isle in the center of the Coliseum so that he could hear more clearly what was going on.

Sampson knew these were the load bearing columns that held up the structure of the Coliseum because he had been there before.

Sampson prayed to God asking God to give him back his strength just one more time and soon he began to push the column's apart and the Coliseum came tumbling down and killed all in attendance instantly that day.

Samson requested that day for God to let him die with the Philistines so the number of the dead Philistines which he slew at his death was more than he had slew during his live.

Samson judged Israel for twenty years.

Even on our present earth today strife and war is still going on between Israel and the Philistine Nation. According to scripture this war has been going on between the countries of Israel and the Philistine Nation since early biblical days and it will not end until God say's enough is enough.

Men and women are still fighting the weakness of sexual desire on our present earth thru the influence of Satan who exploits this weakness in mankind. It still causes a lot of troubles in the lives and marriages of men and women today.

After the death of Samson we find no prominent leaders in Israel for many years. It seemed that the men of Israel did whatever came to their mind which seemed right in their own eyes and there was much fighting between the twelve tribes of Israel.

The Israelites intermarried with other nations and served other gods which God thru Moses had pacifically told the Israeli people not to do.

So for their punishment God let other nations conquer them and they became servants for many years to other nations for their disobedience. After many years of serving other nations, Israel became a nation again on May 14, 1948 as prophesied in Ezekiel Chapter 37 concerning the valley of dry bones that came alive representing the rebirth of the Nation of Israel.

As we fast forward in our journey on our present earth we read of a woman by the name of Naomi. She was married to an Israeli man by the name of Elimelech and they had two sons, Mahlon and Chilion of the province of Bethlehemjudah.

They had traveled to Moab a neighboring country that was founded by Abraham's nephew Lot that we studied about above because of the famine in Bethlehemjudah. During their stay in the country of Moab Naomi's husband died and her two sons had married women from Moab and later her two son's had died also.

Naomi decided to return back to Bethlehemjudah in Israel after she received word that the famine was over in Israel. She invited her two daughters-in-law's to come with her. One daughter-in-law decided to turn back and remain in Moab with her kin. The other daughter-in-law a beautiful lady by the name of Ruth loved Naomi so much that she would not leave her and journeyed with her to Israel and accepted Israel as her country and God as her God.

Later after their arrival back in Bethlehemjudah in the land of Israel, Ruth was gleaning grain for food for her and Naomi in a field owned by a man by the name of Boaz which was a relative of Naomi.

Boaz observing Ruth working in his field asked the young men as to who she was and was told that she was the daughter-in-law of Naomi. Ruth was later introduced to Boaz who was one of Naomi's kinsmen and soon they fell in love and got married. They were blessed with a son and his name was Obed who was the father of a man by the name of Jesse.

Jesse had eight sons. You might ask, just why are we talking about these two men, Obed and Jesse? Maybe you have never heard them mentioned as being prominent men in the Bible but let's find out who they were and what their roles were in our story as we continue our journey on our present earth.

We find in the scriptures that they were very important in the history of Israel. Obed was the grandfather and Jesse was the father to one of the greatest kings mentioned in our Bibles concerning the Nation of Israel.

Remember in the above paragraph we stated that Jesse had eight sons. The youngest son of Jesse was a young shepherd boy by the name of David who would later became King of Israel. Scripture states that David was a man after Gods' own heart. We will study about David later on during our journey on our present earth.

As we continue our journey on our present earth, remember that earlier in our stories of the Bible that I stated that God used some prominent women in the Bible to do his will. Naomi just happens to be one of these women.

Thru the life of Naomi and her daughter-in-law Ruth who married Boaz the linage of Jesus Christ came thru David the eighth son of Jesse we just talked about in the above paragraph. This is all happening because of Gods' plan and love for the Nation of Israel, His chosen nation and people.

You might ask, just how do you know that Israel is God chosen people and nation?

Let's look at the following scripture found in **Deuteronomy 7: [6]** *For thou art an holy people unto the LORD thy God: the LORD thy God hath chosen thee to be a special people unto himself, above all people that are upon the face of the earth.*

This is very plain spoken and if the leaders of the nations on our present earth today would just read and study the Bible for themselves they would see that God chose Israel as His personal nation from among all the nations on earth and the Israeli people are a holy people unto the Lord. Maybe, just maybe things might be different on our present earth today. Is it possible the devil has blinded the minds and eyes of our current leaders, I think so?

Continuing our story about the history of this present earth we read about a priest in Israel by the name of Eli who judged Israel for forty years and one day as he was sitting by the post of the temple as was his custom an Israeli woman by the name of Hannah came to the temple to worship.

Hannah during her worship time was weeping and praying to God in silent prayer just moving her lips not making any noise.

People worship God in many different ways and we should not judge them because they are not worshiping just like we do or the way we think they should worship in a certain way. The important question for all of us is, are we worshiping the true God? Eli while observing her thought she had been drinking and was drunk.

Hannah was actually interceding to God for a child because she was barren and could not have children and she was a reproach as a woman in their society just as Sarah was in our previous story about Abraham.

As she explained to Eli that she was not intoxicated but she was making a petition to God for a certain matter to come to pass, Eli promised her that her request to God would come to pass. Just like God told Abraham and Sarah that Sarah would have a child, Hannah would have a child. God always keeps his word.

Hannah made a vow to God that day if this would come true and she had a son that she would give the child back to God to serve Him all the days of his life.

This is where our custom comes from when many parents have their babies dedicated in our churches. I am sure that many parents never realize that they are agreeing to give their children back to God to do His service for the remainder of their child's life. Sometimes we do things just because we have seen others do this same thing with their children and never realize the spiritual requirement of it.

When the child was weaned, Hannah came back to the temple to worship as was her custom, guess what, she had with her a young son whose name was Samuel just as Eli had promised. True to her vow made to God, she left Samuel with Eli to live and serve in the temple and Samuel later became a great judge and prophet of God in Israel.

Samuel grew and was in favor both to God and man and soon became a great prophet and judge in Israel. Samuel judged Israel most all the days of his adult life.

After Samuel reached a very old age and unable to judge Israel anymore, the people of Israel not being content with having another judge to judge them decided they needed a change.

The Israeli people requested Samuel to speak to God on their behalf and ask God to give them a king to rule over them instead of a priest or prophet so that they could be just like all the other countries around about them. This did not please Samuel who took it personally but when he spoke to God about this God informed Samuel to not take this as a personal attack because the people of Israel were not rejecting Samuel but was rejecting God. This was not the plan of God for Israel to have a king they were to be judged by judges, priests and prophets.

The Israeli people and their leaders did not seek God themselves or consider Gods' will for their lives just like a lot of men and women never do today. Mankind and even churches on our present earth today always wants to be just like everyone else around them, never contented with their life.

Paul said in **Philippians Chapter 4 Verse [11]** *Not that I speak in respect of want: for I have learned, in whatsoever state I am, therewith to be content.*

Ladies and gentlemen we need to be very careful what we request God to grant us during our prayers. It may not be in our best interest or Gods' plan for our lives but sometimes God will grant those prayers and allow what we asked for to come to pass in our lives and then when we get into trouble we place the blame on God for answering our requested prayers. Asking amiss is our fault not Gods'.

Gods' ways are not just best for God, they are also best for us.

God gave the children of Israel their desire which was not according to Gods' plan and directed Samuel to name and anoint a young man by the name of Saul as Israel's first king. Saul was a good looking large muscular man standing head and shoulders above most all the men of Israel.

Remember a few pages up we read in our story about a young man by the name of David who would later become the King of Israel.

Let's look at the life of David. David was a shepherd boy whose job was to take care of his father Jesse's flocks of sheep while growing up. Scripture says in 1Samuel Chapter 16 that David had a ruddy complexion but had a beautiful countenance and goodly to look to. He was also very musical talented and played the flute.

David's seven brothers were very talented warriors but David was only a shepherd boy who played a flute to calm his sheep per the image his brothers saw in him.

David's seven brothers were constantly making fun and looked down on him because he was just a lowly shepherd boy whose lowly job was watching over the sheep which anyone could do.

What they did not know was that David as a young shepherd boy had killed a lion and a bear with his bare hands that had tried to kill his sheep so he was not the timid little shepherd boy his brothers thought he was. He was very skilled in using a slingshot. David had a love for God and had put his trust in God.

The Prophet Samuel was afraid that if King Saul found out that he had anointed one of Jesse's sons as king that Saul would kill him. So God gave instructions to the prophet Samuel to take a heifer and go to Bethlehem to offer a sacrifice to God and invite Jesse and his family to the sacrifice. Samuel was to fill his horn with oil and go anoint one of Jesse's sons as King of Israel because 1Samuel 16: verse one said that God had provided Himself a king from among the sons of Jesse.

Due to the sins of Saul, God informed Samuel that He was going to take the kingship away from Saul and this made the prophet Samuel very sad because of his love for King Saul. God ask Samuel the following question, just how long are you going to morn for Saul, seeing I have rejected him from reigning over Israel? You see, God knows our every thoughts and actions.

Per Samuel request Jesse sent his seven sons before Samuel believing that one of them would surely be anointed king. They were all big good looking men who fought in King Saul's army and Samuel and Jesse both thought that one of them would be the one that God had chosen. God looks on our heart not on our outward appearance.

After all seven brothers had passed by and were rejected by God, Samuel ask Jesse if this was all his sons and was told that the youngest son who was a shepherd boy was watching the sheep herd and Samuel told Jesse to send and fetch him.

When David came in God immediately instructed Samuel to anoint him king because he was the one chosen by God which did not please his seven brothers who were very jealous of David. All the brothers wanted to become king but for the wrong reasons.

Just because David was anointed king of Israel that day, he did not become king immediately.

From this time on scripture states that the Spirit of the Lord came upon David from that day forward.

Soon thereafter there was another war between the nations of Israel and Philistine and David's brothers went to fight the Philistines.

David obeying his father Jesse's instructions was sent to visit some of his brethren on the battlefield who was warriors in the Israeli army. There was a valley which separated the camp of the Israeli armies from the camp of the Philistine armies.

David during this visit listened to one of the Philistine warriors, a giant warrior challenging anyone from the armies of Israel to come down into the valley and fight with him but none would go because all were afraid.

This big giant warrior would come down to the edge of the valley on the Philistines side of the valley where the battle was to take place every morning making fun of the Israeli warriors challenging them to come fight him.

King Saul and all the Israeli soldiers were afraid of him because he was so big, approximately nine feet nine inches tall and what an arm reach.

David's father Jesse had sent him to the battlefield to check on his brethren and to bring them some food.

During his visit David hearing this Philistine giant warrior by the name of Goliath taunting the Israeli soldiers could not understand why no one would go fight this warrior.

David becoming weary of listening to Goliath defying the armies of Israel told those in charge of the army that he would go fight this giant warrior.

Soon it was related to King Saul that there was a young man by the name of David who had agreed to go fight Goliath.

Saul sent for David and offered to let David wear his personal armor but it did not fit so David told King Saul that he could not wear his armor which he had not proven. He would go fight Goliath with his own weapon which he had proven in the past while keeping wild animals away from his father's sheep he was guarding.

Ladies and gentlemen Satan will try to get you to wear his armor but if you are a child of God the armor of Satan just will not fit.

We should put on and wear the whole armor of God as stated in the following scriptures.

Philippians 2: [12] *Wherefore, my beloved, as ye have always obeyed, not as in my presence only, but now much more in my absence, work out* ***your own salvation*** *with fear and trembling.*

Ephesians 6:

[10] *Finally, my brethren, be strong in the Lord, and in the power of his might.*

[11] *Put on the whole armour of God, that ye may be able to stand against the wiles of the devil.*

[12] *For we wrestle not against flesh and blood, but against principalities, against powers, against the rulers of the darkness of this world, against spiritual wickedness in high places.*

[13] *Wherefore take unto you the whole armour of God, that ye may be able to withstand in the evil day, and having done all, to stand.*

[14] *Stand therefore, having your loins girt about with truth, and having on the breastplate of righteousness;*

[15] *And your feet shod with the preparation of the gospel of peace;*

[16] *Above all, taking the shield of faith, wherewith ye shall be able to quench all the fiery darts of the wicked.*

[17] *And take the helmet of salvation, and the sword of the Spirit, which is the word of God:*

[18] *Praying always with all prayer and supplication in the Spirit, and watching thereunto with all perseverance and supplication for all saints;*

I can just hear all of the Israeli warriors laughing and making fun of David when they saw his slingshot and him stooping down and picking five little stones from the brook. This was very embarrassing to the brothers of David for their little brother to offer to fight this giant warrior with a slingshot and five stones.

David's brother Eliab got very upset when he heard David say that he would go fight this giant. Eliab thought if David gets killed our father Jesse will never forgive us and if by chance David killed this giant then it will make me and all my other brothers look like weaklings to all of the other warriors. Pride at work.

As David ran across the valley and drew near to this giant warrior by the name of Goliath this huge soldier started to taunt the Israeli army's again and when he saw David he started cursing him calling him a little boy and telling David that he would feed his flesh to the fowls of the air and to the beasts of the field after he killed him.

These words of Goliath did not scare or bother David at all and David replied to Goliath with the following statement, *Thou comest to me with a sword, and with a spear, and with a shield: but I come to thee in the name of the LORD of hosts, the God of the armies of Israel, whom thou hast defied,* this is found in 1Samuel 17, Verse 45.

David as previously stated had selected five smooth stones from a brook nearby and put them in his shepherd's bag. David reaching into his bag and put one stone into his slingshot and ran toward Goliath. You might ask as to why David selected five stones from the brook, it was because Goliath had four brothers and David was prepared to kill all of them if they came out to fight. David with Gods' help was fearless. We Christians should be this way in fighting the devil.

David who had killed a bear and a lion with his bare hands started whirling the slingshot above his head releasing one side of the slingshot throwing the stone which struck Goliath in the forehead in the only place that had a small opening in Goliath's armor big enough for this stone to go through and it stuck into the forehead of Goliath.

This huge giant warrior fell forward on the ground face down unconscious. David than ran to Goliath and cut off his head with Goliath's own sword and then delivered Goliath's head to King Saul.

James 4: Verse 7 says to ***Resist*** *the devil, and he will flee from you.*

Ladies and gentlemen we cannot resist the devil if we are running away from him we need to run toward the devil instead of away from him.

When the remaining warriors of the army of the Philistines saw their giant warrior Goliath slain they ran for their lives and fled before the warriors of the Israelites and the armies of Israel chased after them and slaughtered many of the Philistine warriors.

God won the battle that day for Israel because of his servant David's obedience.

As a reward King Saul had promised to give anyone who killed this giant warrior many riches along with one of his daughter's in marriage so David became the son-n-law to King Saul.

From the position of a lowly shepherd boy tending sheep elevated to the position of the Kings son-n-law, eating at the Kings table and living in the king's castle all in one day. We see God in action putting David in place to become the anointed King of Israel. God is good.

In the next few years we find King Saul becoming very jealous of David because of David's popularity with the people of Israel. King Saul had promoted David to the position of general over all the Israeli men of war and David was accepted and loved by all the Israeli people along with all of Saul's household.

When David returned home from fighting battles the people would sing the following lyrics, King Saul has killed his thousands but David has killed his ten thousand.

This hurt King Saul's ego and soon he became very angry and jealous so he tried numerous times to kill his son-in-law David who finally had to leave home and flee from King Saul whose actions were not pleasing to God.

David could have killed King Saul on numerous occasions but David would not do this because God had said in **1Chronicles 16: [22]** *Saying, Touch not mine anointed, and do my prophets no harm,* this means with words also not just actions. David had much respect for God and King Saul.

Remember David had already been anointed as the King of Israel many years before by the prophet Samuel even though King Saul was still king.

Gods' plans are completed per Gods' time table not per man's measurement of time.

Ladies and gentlemen we need to be very careful what we say about our leaders and pastors whom God has anointed as the shepherd over His people.

It is God who knows whom He has anointed to do His will not man. God said to pray for those who despitefully use us, not gossiping and talking bad about them. Sometimes this is hard to do, don't you think?

King Saul had disobeyed God so many times that the kingship was taken from him and during a battle with the Philistines he was wounded on the battlefield by archers and he commanded his armor-bearer to kill him but the young man refused to kill him. King Saul took his own sword and fell upon it and was slain by himself.

Soon thereafter David became King of Judah. He reigned for seven years and six months over Judah then later was named King over all of Israel and reigned for a total of forty years uniting Judah and Israel into one nation with one King, God's plan.

Remember God does not change his plans for our lives. Man does this by rejecting Jesus as their Savior. We need to search our lives and ask God to reveal His plan to us during our lives.

David was the eighth son of his father Jesse. The number eight in the bible means a new beginning. The Nation of Israel under the leadership of King David was to have a new beginning.

King David was not a perfect man but scriptures states that he was a man after God's own heart meaning that he had a humble and repentant heart. This was why he was chosen over his brothers whose hearts was not humble and repentant.

After becoming king and leading the armies of Israel thru many wars, King David let sin come into his life by looking at and lusting for another man's wife. He committed adultery with this beautiful lady by the name of Beth-Sheba and she became pregnant. Beth-Sheba was the wife of Uriah a warrior in the army of King David.

If King David would have been on the battlefield with his troops fighting the battle instead of relaxing up on his lofty rooftop looking down onto the roofs of the homes below he would not have seen this beautiful lady Beth-Sheba taking a bath and the sin of sexual lust would not have enter into his mind and heart.

Scripture states that King David sent a messenger to Beth-Sheba requesting her to come to the palace and after much partying together Beth-Sheba spent the night with King David and soon thereafter realized that she had become pregnant. David sent for Uriah to come home and after trying to get him to have sex with Beth-Sheba so they could say the baby was Uriah's but Uriah would not spend the night with Beth-Sheba but stayed all night with the servants in their quarters.

After Uriah returned to the battlefield King David had Beth-Sheba's husband Uriah stationed on the front line of the battlefield hoping for his death by giving instructions for the other warriors to pull away from Uriah leaving him alone and thus he was killed. Another sin of murder added to King David's sinful sexual lust sin.

King David tried very hard to cover up his sins, but God see all and he exposed King David's sin to a prophet by the name of Nathan.

It seems that in life one sin always leads to another sin in trying to cover up the first sin. Soon the prophet Nathan came to see King David and exposed him as the one who had committed these sins against God and Uriah.

King David sought God and asked forgiveness for the sins that he had committed and he was forgiven but he still paid a price for his adulterous sin with Beth-Sheba through his own family and especially his sons. The son born to King David and Beth-Sheba out of wedlock soon died due to their sexual sin.

One of his sons by the name of Absalom even took the kingship away from King David for a short time and became king of Israel himself. Another one of King David's son's raped one of the King David's daughters so you see it does not pay to let sin into our lives as seen in the following scripture.

Deuteronomy 27 [22] *Cursed be he that lieth with his sister, the daughter of his father, or the daughter of his mother. And all the people shall say, Amen.*

You and I will have to pay a price for our sins just like King David even though God will forgive us if we ask in sincerity for His forgiveness in the name of His Son Jesus. We will still have to pay for our sinful wrongs as seen in the verses below found in the book of Romans.

Romans 6: [23] *For the wages of sin is death; but the gift of God is eternal life through Jesus Christ our Lord.*

Romans 14: [12] *So then every one of us shall give account of himself to God.*

The only sin that will not be forgiven is the blasphemy of the Holy Ghost as seen in the following scriptures in the book of Matthew.

Matthew: 12

[31] *Wherefore I say unto you, All manner of sin and blasphemy shall be forgiven unto men: but the blasphemy against the* ***Holy Ghost*** *shall not be forgiven unto men.*

[32] *And whosoever speaketh a word against the Son of man, it shall be forgiven him: but whosoever speaketh against the* ***Holy Ghost****, it shall not be forgiven him, neither in this world, neither in the world to come.*

Modern day Christians who say they believe in the Trinity of the Godhead but are ashamed to call the Holy Ghost by His proper name and still insist that the Holy Spirit and the Holy Ghost are the same just might be close to committing the sin of blaspheming against the Holy Ghost.

Ladies and gentlemen please think about this and be very careful to not do this.

I believe in the Holy Spirit of God. God's Holy Spirit saves us from our sins when we accept His Son Jesus as our Savior. It is the Holy Spirits of God and Jesus manifesting thru the Holy Ghost the third entity of the Godhead who is present all over our present earth.

God who is a Holy Spirit is the first entity of the Godhead so you cannot remove the Holy Spirit from God. We do not call Jesus the Holy Spirit even though He was filled with Gods' Holy Spirit before the Holy Ghost in the form of a dove descended upon Him when He was baptized by John in the river of Jordon. So we should not call the Holy Ghost the Holy Spirit even though the Holy Ghost is made up of Gods' Holy Spirit.

Church we need to get it right, the Trinity Godhead is God the Father, Jesus the Son of God and the Holy Ghost. If it was God, Jesus, Holy Spirit and the Holy Ghost it would not be a trinity Godhead but a quaternary Godhead.

Maybe we should think about why many of our churches today don't have the power of God present and maybe we should start rethinking our own words we use in describing the Holy Ghost as seen in the following scripture.

Acts 10: [38] *How God anointed Jesus of Nazareth with the* ***Holy Ghost*** *and with power: who went about doing good, and healing all that were oppressed of the devil; for God was with him.*

Per the above scripture the anointing and power comes from God working thru the Holy Ghost.

Permit me to do a little teaching on the Holy Ghost. I have been raised in the Pentecostal denomination all my life so I have witnessed some very strange teaching and actions. Many people in the Pentecostal denomination thinks that speaking in an unknown tongue in our public church services is a sign of them being very spiritual but let's look at what Paul who wrote most of our New Testament Bible said about this subject.

1Corinthians:14:

[2] *For he that speaketh in an unknown* ***tongue*** *speaketh not unto men, but unto God: for no man understandeth him; howbeit in the spirit he speaketh mysteries.*

[4] *He that speaketh in an unknown* ***tongue*** *edifieth himself; but he that prophesieth edifieth the church.*

[19] ***Yet in the church I had rather speak five words with my understanding,*** *that by my voice I might teach others also, than ten thousand words in an unknown* ***tongue*.**

[23] *If therefore the whole church be come together into one place, and all speak with* ***tongue****s, and there come in those that are unlearned, or unbelievers, will they not say that ye are mad?*

[26] *How is it then, brethren? when ye come together, everyone of you hath a psalm, hath a doctrine, hath a* ***tongue****, hath a revelation, hath an interpretation. Let all things be done unto edifying.*

There is a gift of interpretation available to those who will seek it.

[27] *If any man speak in an unknown* ***tongue****, let it be by two, or at the most by three, and that by course; and let one interpret.*

What Paul is saying here is that speaking in tongues edifies the one speaking, not the whole church congregation because they will not understand what is being said. To edify the church congregation we need to have an interpretation of these tongues into a language we all can understand. He also states that if unbelievers come in and all they hear is a lot of people speaking in tongues they will think all are mad or crazy and probably get up and leave, thus not receiving what they came for.

Don't get me wrong, I believe in speaking in tongues, which I do speak but mostly during my private prayer time. The power of God is not in the spoken unknown tongue but the power is given by God as we draw close to Him. We need Gods' power to work with the Holy Ghost to become an effective witness unto the unbeliever, praying for the sick believing they will get healed and many other needs would be accomplished.

During my lifetime in the Pentecostal movement most people think you have to speak in an unknown tongue to receive the Holy Ghost but the Holy Ghost was sent to earth to be our comforter and was made available for all mankind when Jesus ascended into Heaven. The spirit of the Holy Ghost was given to all believers and covers the whole universe.

For example the spirit of the Holy Ghost is similar to the air we breathe. We can't see it, we can't taste it, but we know it is everywhere covering the whole earth. It is all around us but until we breathe air into our lungs it has no effect on us. When we breathe air into our lung's we are actually infilling our lungs with air?

As I previously stated the Holy Ghost is all around us, we can't see it, we can't taste it but we know it is present because God Word says God sent the Holy Ghost the third entity of the Godhead to earth to be our comforter at the request of Jesus when He ascended into Heaven to set on His throne at Gods' right hand.

So how do we get the infilling of the Holy Ghost?

It happens when we get our spirit man completely centered on God and we are totally lost in His presence than our spirit man becomes infilled with the Holy Ghost just as our lungs are infilled with air when we breathe. God will speak to us and teach us His Heavenly language then we can converse with Him in His Heavenly language.

The Holy Ghost which is the third entity of the Godhead has been present over all the earth since Jesus requested God to send the Holy Ghost to earth to be our comforter.

Speaking in tongues is not a sign of us receiving the Holy Ghost but it is the sign of the infilling of the Holy Ghost into our spiritual man. Speaking in tongues is one of the gifts made available to us from God when we draw close enough to Him as seen in the following scriptures.

1Corinthians 12:

[4] *Now there are diversities of gifts, but the same Spirit.*

[5] *And there are differences of administrations, but the same Lord.*

[6] *And there are diversities of operations, but it is the same God which worketh all in all.*

[7] *But the manifestation of the Spirit is given to every man to profit withal.*

[8] *For to one is given by the Spirit the word of wisdom; to another the word of knowledge by the same Spirit;*

[9] *To another faith by the same Spirit; to another the gifts of healing by the same Spirit;*

[10] *To another the working of miracles; to another prophecy; to another discerning of spirits;* ***to another divers kinds of tongues;*** *to another the interpretation of tongues:*

[11] *But all these worketh that one and the selfsame Spirit, dividing to every man severally as he will.*

We don't have to prove to the world that we have received this gift. Paul said if we must speak in tongues we should be able to interpret into a language we all can understand. If we want to prove to the world that we have the power given by God working thru the Holy Ghost then we need to be able to use this power given by God to become an effective witness to the unbeliever, praying for the needs of people and seeing the manifestation power of the Holy Ghost in meeting people's needs.

I find in the Pentecostal realms which I have been a part of all my life sometimes we pray for the sick and when they don't receive their healing or have their needs met we often say or think, if we will admit to it, that the one being prayed for does not have enough faith or they must have sin in their lives or it is just not the will of God to answer this prayer at this time, shame on us.

This is only an excuse we use. Is it because we don't have the power of God working thru the Holy Ghost manifesting in us to accomplish getting the needs met for the ones we are praying for? Let's not put all the blame on those being prayed for, where is our faith.

Matthew 3: [11] *I indeed baptize you with water unto repentance: but he that cometh after me is mightier than I, whose shoes I am not worthy to bear: he shall baptize you with the Holy Ghost, and with* ***fire****:*

Fire in the above verse represents POWER that we have been discussing above.

Pastors and ministers if you want the manifestation of the Holy Ghost working in your church seek God for the fire or power to be present and you will see the demonstration power of God working thru the Holy Ghost and people's needs will be met.

I submit the following question, should we be content with just speaking in tongues during our church services being selfish in edifying ourselves without the interpretations or should we be seeking the power that comes from God working thru the Holy Ghost?

I have heard ministers say that we should practice speaking in tongues and some even try to teach you how to speak in tongues but I believe speaking in tongues which is Gods' heavenly language does not need to be taught or practiced. God will help us to speak His language correctly. I believe we should be seeking all of the gifts of the spirit not just speaking in tongues. I believe that speaking in tongues has been abused and misused for many years in the lives of Christians especially in our Pentecostal churches. We should not take the speaking in tongues lightly, it is a Godly language.

Satan the devil does not care if we speak in tongues just so we do not demonstrate the power that comes from God with the Holy Ghost in accomplishing Gods' will.

I ask all of you that still say that Gods' Holy Spirit and the Holy Ghost are the same, in the above verse was Gods' Holy Spirit not present in Jesus before God anointed Him with the Holy Ghost at the river of Jordan when He was baptized by John?

If you answered with a yes and you still insist that the Holy Spirit and the Holy Ghost are the same then why did God have to anoint Jesus with the Holy Ghost as seen in the following scripture if the Holy Spirit which was already in Him and the Holy Ghost are the same?

Luke 3 [**22**] *And the Holy Ghost descended in a bodily shape like a* ***dove*** *upon him, and a voice came from heaven, which said, Thou art my beloved Son; in thee I am well pleased.*

This verse did not say the Holy Spirit descended upon Jesus, it said the Holy Ghost descended upon Him in the form of a Dove.

I encourage Christians to use and read the King James Version of the Bible that was written in the early sixteen hundreds and translated by a large number of scholars who checked and was rechecked to make sure the Bible was translated as close as possible to the original transcripts.

I personally resent the fact that some modern day man with his modern day theology thinks that I am not smart enough to read and understand the words written in the King James Bible. Than some modern day man decides to write new versions of the bible trying to convince and sometimes deceive mankind with his modern day interpretations of the scriptures replacing Gods' interpretations.

By changing one word in a scripture it may change the original thought that God wanted expressed in the original wording of the scripture so be very careful.

If you find the King James Version of the Bible hard to understand just ask God to help you and He will give you the understanding and revelation you need. With man's knowledge on the increase during these end times we should have no trouble understanding the King James Version of the Bible.

Look what God says in Revelation Chapter 22: [18] *For I testify unto every man that heareth the words of the prophecy of this book, If any man shall add unto these things, God shall add unto him the plagues that are written in this book:*

I believe this applies not only adding to this book but also taking away from or changing the word of God written in our bibles.

If you do not agree with me that is between you and God as seen in the following scripture:

Philippians2: [12] *Wherefore, my beloved, as ye have always obeyed, not as in my presence only, but now much more in my absence, work out your own salvation with fear and trembling.*

Pastors and teachers if we are not careful the generations following us will not even know who or what the Holy Ghost is. Satan will use anything he can to discredit the true Trinity of the Godhead made up of God the Father, Jesus the Son and the Holy Ghost sometimes by distorting the scriptures in the modern translations of the Bible.

Back to our story of King David:

After the death of Uriah and the mourning period was over for Beth-Sheba, King David brought Beth-Sheba to his house and took Beth-Sheba as his wife as he should have done and later they had a son by the name of Solomon who became King of Israel when his father King David died.

Jesus' earthly father Joseph and mother Mary came thru the linage of King David down thru his son Solomon. The generations of Jesus are found in the book of Matthew, Chapter One and in Luke Chapter 3, verses 23 thru 38.

King David always wanted to build God a temple in Israel and had accumulated a lot of materials to build it with but God would not allow David to build his temple because David was a warrior who had taken many lives and had committed the sexual sin with Beth-Sheba, but God did let David's son Solomon build Him the temple as we will study later.

King Saul, King David and King Solomon each reigned over Israel for forty years.

The number forty in our bible represents a period of testing, trial or probation or the generation of man.

King Solomon was a good king to the people of Israel and he reigned over Israel for forty years. As a reward for being so good to Gods' people, God told him in 1Kings Chapter 3 Verse Five to ask for anything he wanted and He would grant it to him. King Solomon asked God in verse nine to give him wisdom and understanding to judge the Nation of Israel so that he could discern between good and evil. God said in verse eleven, because thou hast asked this thing, and hast not asked for thyself long life neither hast asked riches for thyself, nor hast asked the life of thine enemies, but hast asked for thyself understanding to discern judgement behold I have done according to thy words.

God not only gave him wisdom and understanding that scripture says exceeded much but scripture says that God also gave him a wise, understanding and largeness of heart **(wisdom and understanding)** even as the sand that is on the sea shore and rewarded him for not asking for selfish personal riches by making him very wealthy, probably the riches man to ever live on our present earth.

God told Solomon that there shall not be any other king like you and that God would lengthen his days.

Even though King Solomon was a very good king for many years to the Nation of Israel he had a weakness that a lot of men have today, he liked women as seen in the following scriptures.

1Kings: 11

[1] *But king Solomon* ***love****d many strange women, together with the daughter of Pharaoh, women of the Moabites, Ammonites, Edomites, Zidonians, and Hittites;*

[2] *Of the nations concerning which the LORD said unto the children of Israel, Ye shall not go in to them, neither shall they come in unto you: for surely they will turn away your heart after their gods: Solomon clave unto these in* ***love****.*

King Solomon had 700 wives (Princesses) and 300 concubines (secondary wives) which became his downfall in his later years by persuading him to worship their pagan gods instead of the true God and this was in direct rebellion to the law given by God to Moses, so later in the life of King Solomon he also paid the consequences for his sins.

King Solomon was the king that God allowed to build Him the first Temple in Jerusalem for the Nation of Israel in the Tenth Century B.C. instead of his father David. It was a magnificent structure. King Solomon did not spare any expense in the building and furnishing of this temple. Rulers from many nations came to see it. God's Shekinah glory filled this temple, God was pleased.

After King Solomon died there were a number of kings who reigned over Israel, some served and worshiped God while others did evil in the sight of God.

As we continue our journey on our present earth we find one such king who was an evil king by the name of Ahab who was married to an evil woman by the name of Jezebel. They served and worshipped a god by the name of Baal.

Remember we discussed a man earlier in our journey that lived on our present earth by the name of Nimrod who also served this same god and was the grandson of Noah's son Ham. This religion of Baal although called by another name in today's society is still very prevalent in our world today. Many of our leaders living on our Our Present Earth today being influenced and deceived by Satan are beginning to portray it as a peaceful religion on our present earth and encouraging mankind to accept it as just another way to worship God.

This is a religion devised by Satan and is still very active and real in our society today. It may be called by another name but it is still the same evil counterfeit religion with radical religionist men and women trying to force men and women living on our present earth to accept this religion in worshiping man instead of the one true God.

Sometimes the penalty for not accepting and endorsing this religion and denouncing the Christian faith is death by beheading or shot to death as seen on our televisions today.

I believe this will be the counterfeit religion of the antichrist administered thru his religionist system and forced upon the people of this earth during the seven year tribulation period.

This religion will be endorsed by the false prophet; the leader of the One World Church who I think will be the Pope of the Roman Catholic Church. Why the Pope you might ask, because the antichrist will be the leader of the revived Roman Empire made up from ten Middle Eastern Nations during the Seven Year Tribulation Period and he will use the Pope to deceive as many members of the Catholic Church to accept this religion as possible. You might want to read my book titled **The Final Destination of Man** to study more on this subject.

As we continue our journey on this present earth we find God had a prophet by the name of Elijah who was a constant thorn in the lives of Ahab and Jezebel.

Ahab reigned over Israel for twenty two years and scripture states that Ahab did more to provoke the Lord God of Israel to anger then all the kings of Israel that were before him. For being so evil God sent Elijah to inform Ahab that it would not rain for three year and six months in Ahab's kingdom for punishment for his evil ways and it did not rain, reference to this is found in 1Kings Chapter 17.

Food became in short supply, drinking water was running out and the earth was dry and very dusty. Ahab and Jezebel being very upset and angry blamed Elijah for all their troubles.

During this time God instructed Elijah to go eastward and hide by the brook Che'-rith that is beyond Jordon. God told Elijah to drink from this brook and that He would send ravens that would bring Elijah bread and flesh in the morning and in the evening to feed him there.

Have you ever wondered where those ravens got this bread and flesh? I think God sent these ravens into Ahab's palace and the ravens took bread and meat from off of Ahab's table or out of the kitchen and brought to Elijah for him to eat. Scripture states that the wealth of the wicked is laid up for the righteous; this could mean a supply of food instead of monetary supply.

After a while scripture says that this brook dried up so God sent Elijah to a city called Zarephath unto a widow woman. When Elijah got to the city of Zarephath he saw this widow woman gathering a few sticks to make a fire to cook one last cake of bread for her and her son to eat and then with no more food in the house they would die due to the famine in the land caused by no rain.

Elijah requested that she give him some water to drink and to cook him some food to eat. Remember she only had enough meal and oil for one cake of bread which she was going to fix for her and her son to eat and then they would die.

In obedience to Elijah the prophet, she gave Elijah some water to drink and she cooked him her last cake of bread and then to her surprise when she looked into the meal barrel and into the cruse of oil there was enough meal and oil to cook food for her and her son as seen in the following scripture.

1Kings 17 Verse 14: *For thus saith the LORD God of Israel, The barrel of meal shall not waste, neither shall the cruse of oil fail, until the day that the LORD sendeth rain upon the earth.*

It was three years and six months before it rained again as seen in the following scripture:

James 5: 17: *Elias was a man subject to like passions as we are, and he prayed earnestly that it might not rain: and it rained not on the earth by the space of three years and six months.* This widow woman never ran out of oil and meal for three years and six months due to her respecting and obeying the words of the man of God the Prophet Elijah.

Queen Jezebel, Ahab's wife whose name meant "where is the prince" talking about Baal hated Elijah. She had tried to kill all of Gods' prophets but a man by the name of Obadiah had hid 100 prophets in a cave and fed them with bread and water.

Jezebel thought if only I could figure out a way to kill Elijah everything would be wonderful again since he is the one causing Israel's troubles.

Satan always blames someone else for the trouble he causes. Jezebel thought, maybe my prophets of Baal can figure out a way to get rid of him. They were willing to do this, because they knew that she would reward them with many pleasures in life if they succeeded.

The devil is always trying to kill Christians and will promise you many pleasures in life if you will follow him but scripture says that following the devil only leads down the road to destruction but God is our protector, supplier and He is never off duty and if we follow God scripture says that His road leads to everlasting life.

Christians if you should get killed, just think you will be immediately in the presence of God asleep in Jesus in Paradise waiting for the Catching up of the Church. Not a bad place to be.

After the building of an alter to sacrifice to their god the prophets of Baal tried very hard to get into contact with their god Baal all day long so that they could kill Elijah wanting to please their Queen Jezebel but Baal never answered. Later that day God turned the table on these false prophets.

Elijah mocked and made fun of these prophets of Baal until noon and then until the time for Elijah's evening sacrifice telling them that maybe their god had gone on a long journey, or maybe he was asleep or busy talking and could not hear their cries.

Elijah encouraged them to call and scream more loudly to try to wake up their god Baal because he surely must be asleep. After cutting and hurting themselves all day long with no response from their god Baal the altar was broken down due to their screaming, stomping and jumping up and down on it.

Elijah had to repair the altar broken down by these prophets during their calling on their god Baal before he could offer his sacrifice to the true God.

To the surprise of the four hundred and fifty prophets of Baal, Elijah then dug a trench around the altar holding Elijah's sacrifice and poured eight barrels of water over the bullock that he was offering to God as a sacrifice and the water ran off the altar and filled up the trench and then Elijah called upon God and scriptures said God sent fire down from Heaven and burned up the sacrifice, the wood, the altar stones, the dust and licked up the water in the trenches thus making Himself known to the people of Israel as the one and only true God.

Per Gods' instructions, Elijah killed all of Jezebel's four hundred and fifty prophets of Baal that evening after they had called on their god Baal all day long, cutting themselves on the altar asking Baal to accept their sacrifice.

When King Ahab's wife Jezebel received word that Elijah had killed all of her prophets she became so angry and upset that she screamed and cried all night long and made a vow to not rest until she had Elijah killed. No peace or sleep for King Ahab and all his servants that night. The following scripture fits this situation.

Proverbs 25: [24] *It is better to dwell in the corner of the housetop, than with a brawling woman and in a wide house.*

She even sent a message to Elijah telling him his life would end just like the lives of her prophets of Baal. She tried and tried to kill Elijah but God protected Elijah.

God pronounced judgment on evil Queen Jezebel, just as He will on all un-believers' who rejects Jesus as their Savior soon on judgment day on our present earth. Gods' judgments are real, what He says He will do He will do.

One day soon thereafter as Jezebel was looking out the upstairs window of their palace leaning out over the window sill overlooking their kingdom screaming at the people on the streets below and looking to see if she could spot Elijah in town that during her rage someone threw her out of the window in the king's palace and scripture says the dogs dismantled her body and licked up her blood as seen in the following scripture.

2Kings 9: [10] *And the dogs shall eat* ***Jezebel*** *in the portion of Jezreel, and there shall be none to bury her. And he opened the door, and fled.*

Gods' judgments are real. What He says He will do, He will do. It will come to pass.

As we continue our story concerning our present earth we find the prophet Elijah meeting a young man by the name of Elisha who had left his family and all he had and followed Elijah where ever he went.

Elijah tried to get Elisha to stay away from him but Elisha recognizing the Spirit of God working in Elijah would not leave him because he desired to have that same spirit in himself. Elisha made up his mind to follow Elijah everywhere he went because of his desire for Gods' spirit to be in his life.

Finally one day Elijah getting a little frustrated could not stand it anymore so he turned and asked Elisha, just what is it that you want from me? Elisha said that he wanted a double portion of Elijah's Godly Spirit to be upon him.

What a request. We should all desire a double portion of Gods' Spirit to be upon us. We can have this if we are willing to do the following.

1Thessalonians 5:

[**16**] *Rejoice evermore.*

[**17**] *Pray without ceasing.*

[**18**] *In everything give thanks: for this is the will of God in Christ Jesus concerning you.*

[**19**] *Quench not the Spirit.*

[**20**] *Despise not prophesyings.*

[**21**] *Prove all things; hold fast that which is good.*

[**22**] *Abstain from all appearance of evil.*

Elijah's response was that if Elisha saw him when he was taken away from this present earth he would drop his mantle and if Elisha caught Elijah's mantle as it floated back to our present earth that he could have this double portion of the Godly Spirit of Elijah.

I think God and Elijah must have had a conversation concerning this before God took Elijah up in a whirlwind from this present earth.

Elisha never left Elijah's side after Elijah told him this. Elisha did see Elijah when he was taken away by God from our present earth in a whirlwind riding in a chariot of fire drawn with horses of fire and he caught Elijah's mantle when Elijah dropped it as it floated back to our present earth.

God gave Elisha his desires, a double portion of Elijah's Godly Spirit.

The first test to the power of God that Elisha did after catching the mantle of Elijah was when he came to a river of water that he needed to cross he struck the water with Elijah's mantle and said, where is the Lord God of Elijah and scripture says the waters parted and he went over to the other side.

Elisha became another one of the great prophets to the Nation of Israel.

As we continue our journey and after many more kings in Israel we come to a king by the name of Hezekiah and another prophet in Israel by the name of Isaiah.

Israel is at war with Assyria and Sennacherib the king of Assyria sends word to Hezekiah telling him what he intends to do to him and Israel if Israel does not surrender to his armies.

Satan the devil likes to brag about what he can do to us but he can only do what God allows him to do.

Christians don't be afraid of Satan the devil. Scriptures state that he goes about as a roaring lion. He just makes a lot of noise like a roaring lion. His bark is worse than his bite. He can only afflict our mortal body not our Godly spirit.

God did not like this message that this Assyrian King Sennacherib sent to King Hezekiah so He sent an angel **(probably the archangel Michael the commander of God armies)** who smites the camp of the Assyrians and kills one hundred eighty five thousand Assyrian warriors. This quickly got the attention of King Sennacherib of Assyria who departs from Israel immediately and heads toward home and was later killed by two of his own sons Adrammelech and Sharezer with a sword.

It does not pay to threaten God or His people. God does take care of us.

The scripture says in: 2Peter 3: [9] *The Lord is not slack concerning his promise, as some men count slackness; but is longsuffering to us-ward, not willing that any should perish, but that all should come to repentance.*

As we continue our story we find that King Hezekiah has become very sick and is near death. God sends the prophet Isaiah to tell him to get his house in order because he was going to die and not live. What a message to give to a king, you could be beheaded or thrown into prison for speaking these words during this time on our present earth.

I wonder what we would do if our pastor came to our home and told us that God had just sent him to tell us to get our house in order that we were going to die.

Would we immediately go to prayer like King Hezekiah did and have faith and put our trust in God to answer our prayers or would we just laugh and brush it off thinking that our pastor must have ate or drank too much which effected his mind or surely he must be wrong and listening to the wrong voice?

The Bible says that King Hezekiah turned himself to the wall and prayed to God and God added fifteen more years to his life. Hezekiah in turning toward the wall shut out all distractions, he was focusing on God only.

God answered King Hezekiah prayer and God is still in the prayer answering business today. It is so easy to get distracted while praying, that is why we need to pray in the Holy Ghost, God's Heavenly Language which the devil cannot understand as seen in the following scripture.

Ephesians 3: [20] *Now unto him* ***(God)*** *that is able to do exceeding abundantly above all that we ask or think, according to the power* ***(of the Holy Ghost)*** *that worketh in us.*

As we continue our journey on our present earth we read about a Babylonian King by the name of King Nebuchadnezzar coming to fight against Israel and defeating Israel.

You might ask as to why Israel was always being defeated by other nations. It was because of the leadership of the Israeli Nation turning from God and leading the people away from God just like the leaders in our nation's are doing today on our present earth.

God will pronounce judgment against our nation's if our leaders and people continue to defy God just as He did to Israel as seen in the following scripture.

Romans Chapter 2, Verse [11] *For there is no respect of persons* ***(or nations)*** *with God.*

Among the captives taken from Israel to Babylon the capitol city of King Nebuchadnezzar's Babylonian Empire which today would be the modern nation of Iraq, were four young men by the names of Daniel, Hananiah, Mishael and Azariah of the tribe of Judah, in our language today they would be called POW's.

These four young men loved and served God and decided that they would not eat food from the king's table even thought it was the best of food available but it would have defiled them.

They were in prison at this time but God gave them favor with those in charge while they were incarcerated. They requested that the prison warden give them pulse (beans or vegetables) to eat and water to drink for ten days and if they did not appear more fairer in complexion then those who were eating from the kings table than they would eat whatever the warden gave them to eat.

Guess what, their complexion appeared far better than any of the others who had eaten from the Kings table and they never had to eat the Kings food. If we will take a stand for God, God will always come thru for us.

God gave them knowledge and skill in all learning and wisdom more than all the wise men of Babylon. God also gave Daniel understanding in all visions and dreams.

As we continue our story we find that King Nebuchadnezzar of the Babylonian Empire had a dream and in his dream he saw a large statue approximately 90 feet high and 9 feet wide.

This statue was an image of a man whose head was made of gold, the chest and arms made of silver, the belly and thighs made of brass, and the legs made of iron, feet and toes made part iron and clay.

The gold head represented the Babylonian Empire, the modern nation of Iraq.

The chest and arms of silver represented the Medes-Persian Empire, the modern nation of Iran.

The belly and thighs of brass represented the Grecian Empire, the modern nation of Greece.

The two legs of iron **(one leg represents the old Roman Empire which was located in the modern nation of Italy and the other leg represents the revived Roman Empire made up from Ten Middle Eastern Nations which I believe to be Muslim Nations which will make up Satan's empire during the tribulation period.** The feet and ten toes part iron and clay represents the kings or leaders of these ten nations.

These four empires represents the ruling time of the gentile nations on this present earth from the time of King Nebuchadnezzar approximately 600 BC until the beginning time of the One Thousand Year Millennium and the reign of Jesus when He returns to our present earth to set up the Kingdom of God.

King Nebuchadnezzar called all the Magicians, the Astrologers, the Sorcerers and the Chaldeans in his kingdom to interpret his dream but they could not give the interpretation of his dream. Later King Nebuchadnezzar had this statue actually built on the outskirts of his city Babylon.

This great Babylonian Empire was founded by King Nebuchadnezzar in the early 600 BC and consisted of multiple nations and regions conquered under his leadership. King Nebuchadnezzar was the first great Gentile leader and scripture focuses on this Gentile system all the way to the Return of Christ at the beginning of the One Thousand Year Millennium.

Daniel the great prophet was a Hebrew POW of this King. The king being very upset because no one could interpret his dream gave an order for all the magicians, astrologers, sorcerers and wise men to be destroyed which would include Daniel, Hananiah, **(Shadrach),** Mishael **(Meshach),** and Azariah **(Abednego)**.

Daniel quickly asked to have a meeting with the King and asked for a little time and he would give the King the interpretation to his dream. Daniel went home and prayed to his God and soon God gave him the interpretation of this dream to give to the King. King Nebuchadnezzar recognizing Daniel's spiritual ability to interrupt dreams made him ruler over all the magicians, astrologers, sorcerers and Chaldeans of the kingdom.

These magicians, astrologers, sorcerers and Chaldeans of Nebuchadnezzar's kingdom even though Daniel saved their lives did not appreciate Daniel a Hebrew POW ruling over them and telling them what to do besides being very jealous of Daniel for his ability to understand and interpret dreams. They tried to find fault with Daniel so that they could accuse him to the king to get him demoted or even killed.

Later after King Nebuchadnezzar had this statue of a man constructed, he issued a decree that all the leaders in his government should come to see this statue and all should bow down and worship this golden statue of his when they heard the sound of his music.

The three Hebrew boys, Hananiah, **(Shadrach),** Mishael **(Meshach),** and Azariah **(Abednego)** would not bow down and King Nebuchadnezzar got so angry that he had them thrown into the fiery furnace which was heated seven times hotter than it was designed to be heated.

This furnace was so hot that the men that had bound and threw these three Hebrew men into the furnace at the kings command was killed by the flames coming out of the furnace.

These three Hebrew boys were not hurt by the fire at all because scripture says that King Nebuchadnezzar looked into the furnace and saw a fourth man walking with the three Hebrew boys in the flames of the fiery furnace and King Nebuchadnezzar said to those around him that this man looked like the Son of God.

Have you ever wondered how this Gentile King knew what the Son of God looked like, I have? Maybe Daniel had related to him about God answering his prayer or just the life that Daniel lived was a Godly example that the King recognized.

I believe all mankind whether they will admit it or not know that God is our creator just like King Nebuchadnezzar did.

After the death of King Nebuchadnezzar, his grandson Belshazzar was acting as King while Belshazzar's father King Nabonidus who had married one of King Nebuchadnezzar's daughters became King but was on a journey away from Babylon.

During King Nabonidus' absence Belshazzar gave a banquet for all the generals, wives, concubines and other important people in his kingdom. During this banquet with a lot of eating, drinking and partying going on during the night with the party getting wilder and wilder, Belshazzar feeling very important and secure instructed his servants to bring the sacred temple vessels that his grandfather King Nebuchadnezzar had brought to Babylon from the temple in Israel so that he and his guest could use them to drink and eat from during this banquet and wild party.

As they were eating and drinking from these sacred temple vessels and praising the god of metal and wood a hand appeared and started writing on the wall. This got Belshazzar's and all those attending his banquet attention very quickly.

All drinking and partying stopped. The party came to a screeching halt. You could have heard a pin drop on the floor.

Ever one's eyes were now focused on the hand that was writing on the wall. Those that were drunk became instantly sober; No one was hungry or thirsty anymore.

Belshazzar's knees began knocking against each other, his heart was pounding and his blood pressure increased and he was becoming very faint. No one had ever witness anything like this before. What did it mean, how could a hand just appears out of nowhere and began writing on the wall?

In his confused and stupor mind Belshazzar made a decree that he would make the man who could read and interpret this writing on the wall the third ruler in the kingdom.

The first ruler was King Nabonidus, second ruler was King Belshazzar and the third ruler was to be the one who could interpret the hand writing on the wall.

Not one of his magicians, wise men or astrologers could read this writing even though many tried so finally Belshazzar's grandmother, King Nebuchadnezzar's wife remembered that there was a man by the name of Daniel one of the Hebrew POW had interpreted King Nebuchadnezzar's dream of the great statue of a man.

Daniel was located and called in quickly. He gave the interpretation that King Belshazzar was found guilty of not giving praise to God and was guilty for using the sacred temple vessels to eat and drink from that was brought from the temple in Jerusalem by his grandfather King Nebuchadnezzar and before night was over the kingdom would be taken from him and so it was.

Belshazzar made Daniel the third ruler in the kingdom even though Daniel told him to keep his gifts.

That night the Babylonian Kingdom now the modern nation of Iraq was defeated by the Medes-Persian Kingdom call Persia in our Bible which is now the modern nation of Iran. This Medes-Persian kingdom came into power which represented the chest and arms of silver of King Nebuchadnezzar's statue of a man.

Daniel 5: [31] says, *And Darius the Median took the kingdom, being about threescore and two years* ***(62)*** *old.*

As we continue our journey on our present earth we find God giving Daniel favor with this new Medes-Persian empire and its leaders but not with the magicians and sorcerers of this kingdom. They soon became very jealous of Daniel and tried to get him killed by tricking the King into signing a decree concerning praying to any other god but to the gods of the Medes-Persians for thirty days.

I much rather have the favor of God in my life like Daniel than favor of man. Many people love the praise **(favor)** of man today on our present earth more than of God. Don't be one of these for God will pass judgment on you just like he did to these magicians and sorcerers during Daniel's time.

These magicians and sorcerers knew that Daniel prayed to his God three times a day and knew he would not stop even though the King had signed a decree that no one could pray to any other god than the god of the Medes-Persians for thirty days.

Soon they found Daniel praying to God just as he always did thus defying the Kings decree.

They were so happy and proud of themselves thinking that they had finally devised a plan to get rid of Daniel and immediately brought to the Kings attention that Daniel was praying to his God in defiance to the Kings' decree.

The King realizing that he had been tricked became very sorrowful and depressed. He stayed up all night trying to figure out a way to keep Daniel from being thrown into the lion's den but knew that he had to honor his word.

The next evening Daniel was thrown into the den of lions but God shut up the lion's mouths. I believe that these lions became so tame that Daniel may have used one of them to lay his head on while sleeping.

On Gods' New Earth all animals will be tame as seen in the following scripture.

Isaiah 11: [6] *The wolf also shall dwell with the lamb, and the leopard shall lie down with the kid; and the calf and the young lion and the fatling together; and a little child shall lead them.*

Wow, this will be just one of the great things we get to enjoy on Gods' New Earth. I have always wanted to pet some of Gods' created creatures which is not possible on our present earth today. Is this something you would like to do also, if so all you have to do is accept Jesus as you Savior and it will be possible?

The next day very early in the morning the King came to the opening of the lion's den and speaking very loudly called out, Daniel was the God whom you serve able to deliver you from the lion's? Daniel replied, Oh King live forever.

The King became very excited and ordered Daniel to be released immediately from the den of lions. Than the King had all the magicians, sorcerers along with their families thrown into the den of lions and they were all mauled and killed by the lions.

It does not pay to falsely accuse or do wrong to God's people. God sees and will judge and repay you.

Proverbs Chapter 15: [3] *The eyes of the LORD are in every place, beholding the evil and the good.*

The Medes-Persian Empire was later defeated by the Grecian Empire which represented the belly and thighs of brass led by a general by the name of Alexander.

This story is described in Daniel Chapter 8 which talks about a ram with two horns in verse twenty which represented the dual kingship of the Media-Persia Empire a dual empire now the modern nation of Iran and a goat with one horn which represented the king of the Grecia Empire now the modern nation of Greece which destroys the ram in verse twenty one.

General Alexander of the Grecian Empire died at the age of thirty three leaving no blood kinsmen to succeed him on his throne so his empire was divided between his four mercenary generals from the following countries Egypt, Thrace which is Bulgaria, Macedonia and Syria.

Daniel 8:23 says: *And in the latter time of their kingdom, when the transgressors are come to the full, a king of fierce countenance, and understanding dark sentences, shall stand up.*

This king of a fierce countenance in the above verse was a man by the name of Antiochus that bible history records as being a very heinous character who is a forerunner of the antichrist who will also be a heinous character and will come to power during the end times called the Seven Year Tribulation Period found in the book of Revelation in our Bible which I believe is going to be very soon.

We don't hear much in the news today about the first three countries, sometimes Egypt, but Syria is in the news every day on our present earth. I believe Syria will be one of the countries that play's a major role during the Seven Year Tribulation End Times on our present earth.

I am convinced that the antichrist will be a descendent of Syria. I believe this country will be part of the Ten Middle Eastern Nations that will make up Satan's empire, the first beast of Revelation Chapter 13.

You might ask, why do you believe this? This is because the antichrist as a Syrian is a half-brother to the Israelis. Remember all of Abraham's sons who fathered many nations we talked about in the story of Abraham above. Syria is one of those nations.

This man who will later become the antichrist is such a gifted politician that Israel will accept and put their faith in this leader and Israel will be enticed and deceived into accepting a seven year peace treaty devised by him. Read my book, **The Final Destination of Man** for more on this subject.

This Grecian Empire was later defeated by the Roman Empire which represents the two legs of iron of King Nebuchadnezzar's statue. These two legs represents the Old Roman Empire and the New Revived Roman Empire which will be made up from Ten Middle Eastern Nations and the ten toes are made up of iron and clay which represents the ten leaders of these nations that make up the first beast of the Book of Revelation Chapter 13.

This colossal image of King Nebuchadnezzar's is a symbol that represents the ruling Gentile kingdoms during the times of the Gentiles from the reign of King Nebuchadnezzar unto the time when the antichrist and his armies are destroyed never to rise again at the battle at Armageddon by Jesus Christ the King of Kings.

After this battle fought at Armageddon Jesus will establish and rule the earthly Kingdom of God during the One Thousand Year Millennium on our present earth.

After these four kingdoms Gods' Word states in the following scriptures that a stone was cut out of the mountain without hands and it would come and destroy the above mentioned image.

Daniel 2 :[45] *Forasmuch as thou sawest that the stone was cut out of the mountain without hands, and that it brake in pieces the iron, the brass, the clay, the silver, and the gold; the great God hath made known to the king what shall come to pass hereafter: and the dream is certain, and the interpretation thereof sure.*

That stone is none other than Jesus Christ and the earthly Kingdom of God that will later be located on our present earth during the One Thousand Year Millennium and will have no ending but will be established for eternity and later this earthly Kingdom of God will be located on Gods' New Earth created after the One Thousand Year Millennium which we will discuss later on in our book.

On our present earth it seems that Christian believers are living in some of the same conditions as Daniel and his friends were as captives of King Nebuchadnezzar in Babylon.

The world leaders of our present earth today have but one desire, to have a one-world government and a one-world religion that will rule all nations. The leaders of our present earth are striving to create a one world governing system to rule this present earth which belongs to God, with the fullness thereof but will never succeed.

Earthly leaders are attempting to do away with individual nations and force every nation and human beings on our present earth to pledge allegiance to one single political authority ruled by the one world government whose leader will be the antichrist.

They also want to do away with all religious organizations and force Christian Church Leaders to sign a form of allegiance to a single religious authority called the one world church.

As we continue our journey on this present earth we come to the birth of Jesus Christ who was a descendent of King David of the tribe of Judah. Jesus was a real person with a real earthly body even thought His was of divine decent and he did actually live on this present earth that we live on.

Ladies and gentlemen these stories in this book are about real people who lived real lives on our real present earth.

The Roman Empire was the ruling authority over Israel during the life of Jesus on our present earth.

Luke 1: Talking about the birth of Jesus:

[26] *And in the sixth month the angel Gabriel was sent from God unto a city of Galilee, named Nazareth.*

[27] *To a virgin espoused to a man whose name was Joseph, of the house of David; and the virgin's name was Mary.*

[28] *And the angel came in unto her, and said, Hail, thou that art highly favoured, the Lord is with thee: blessed art thou among women.*

[29] *And when she saw him, she was troubled at his saying, and cast in her mind what manner of salutation this should be.*

[30] *And the angel said unto her, Fear not, Mary: for thou hast found favour with God.*

[31] *And, behold, thou shalt conceive in thy womb, and bring forth a son, and shalt call his name JESUS.*

[32] *He shall be great, and shall be called the Son of the Highest: and the Lord God shall give unto him the throne of his father David:*

[33] *And he shall reign over the house of Jacob forever; and of his kingdom there shall be no end.*

[34] *Then said Mary unto the angel, How shall this be, seeing I know not a man?*

[35] *And the angel answered and said unto her, The Holy Ghost shall come upon thee, and the power of the Highest shall overshadow thee: therefore also that holy thing which shall be born of thee shall be called the Son of God.*

Isaiah also prophesied concerning Jesus as the Son of God some seven hundred years before Jesus was born as seen in the following scriptures.

Isaiah: 11

[1] *And there shall come forth a rod out of the stem of Jesse, and a Branch shall grow out of his roots:*

[2] *And the spirit of the LORD shall rest upon him, the spirit of wisdom and understanding, the spirit of counsel and might, the spirit of knowledge and of the fear of the LORD;*

[3] *And shall make him of quick understanding in the fear of the LORD: and he shall not judge after the sight of his eyes, neither reprove after the hearing of his ears:*

[4] *But with righteousness shall he judge the poor, and reprove with equity for the meek of the earth: and he shall smite the earth with the rod of his mouth, and with the breath of his lips shall he slay the wicked.*

God had chosen Mary to be the mother of Jesus but He also chose Joseph to be the earthly father of Jesus. In the book of Matthew we find that scriptures state that Joseph was a righteous, kind and sensitive man.

As the fiancé of Mary's he could have divorce Mary when he found out that she was with child. Mary would have faced disgrace and could have even been stoned to death.

Josephs' initial reaction probably was to break the engagement but due to God sending an angel to visit him he acted very kindly to Mary even though family and friends may have publicly humiliated him but he followed Gods' instructions given by the angel and was a very good father to Jesus raising Him in the Jewish traditions and spiritual observances.

The last time that we read about Joseph as Jesus' earthly father in scripture was when Joseph, Mary and family traveled to Jerusalem from Nazareth as were their custom every year for the Feast of the Passover.

Jesus being twelve years old had remained behind talking with the religionist leader in the temple after his parents Joseph and Mary had begun their journey home.

It is very possible that Joseph died sometime before Jesus began His Ministry at the age of thirty. The Bible just does not say any more about him.

At the time of the birth of Jesus, the gift of the Holy Ghost had not yet been sent to earth and given to all mankind as it is today and was not present in most of the lives of people of that time period living on our present earth. It was only given to men and women on special occasions as it was with Mary the mother of Jesus.

The Holy Ghost was sent by God to be our comforter and given to men on our present earth on the Day of Pentecost in the upper room after the death and resurrection of Jesus and remains on our present earth today as our comforter and guide as seen in the following scriptures.

Acts 2:

[1] *And when the day of Pentecost was fully come, they were all with one accord in one place.*

[2] *And suddenly there came a sound from heaven as of a rushing mighty wind, and it filled all the house where they were sitting.*

[3] *And there appeared unto them cloven tongues like as of fire, and it sat upon each of them.*

[4] *And they were all filled with the Holy Ghost, and began to speak with other tongues, as the Spirit gave them utterance.*

I believe these men and women were already saved by Gods' Holy Spirit living within them but in the above verses they were all filled with the Holy Ghost and with this infilling of the Holy Ghost they spoke with Gods' Heavenly language.

Just another example of the difference between Gods' Holy Spirit and the Holy Ghost.

The Holy Ghost was sent from God and is available to all believers on our present earth today with the opportunity of the infilling into our spirit the evidence of speaking in Gods' heavenly language to all who believe in the fullness of the Trinity of the Godhead.

Mary the mother of Jesus just accepted and believed the words of the angel Gabriel concerning this message sent from God.

We need to learn to trust and believe God in our lives on this present earth today just as Mary did.

Matthew 1: [18] *Now the birth of Jesus Christ was on this wise: When as his mother Mary was espoused to Joseph, before they came together, she was found with child of the Holy Ghost.*

For those of you who don't believe in the Holy Ghost as the third person of the Godhead, did you know that the Holy Ghost is actually the father of Jesus? This is what it says in the above scripture verse eighteen, not my words but the Word of God.

Luke 1:

[37] *For with God nothing shall be impossible.*

[38] *And Mary said, Behold the handmaid of the Lord;* ***be it unto me according to thy word.*** *And the angel departed from her.*

Ladies and gentlemen we need to have the same mindset as Mary stated in Verse 38, *BE IT UNTO ME ACCORDING TO THY WORD.*

We humans living on this present earth today need to stop trying to figure God out per our own understanding and ask Him for His understanding and just accept Him at His Word.

If we would do this, maybe we would get a lot more of our prayers answered, don't you think?

God desires pure actions but even more He desires pure motives for our actions.

One day as I was meditating and thinking about God and how God must have felt when He looked down upon this present earth from the balcony of Heaven into a city called Bethlehem and saw a little baby boy laying in a manger who was conceived by the Holy Ghost to a virgin girl by the name of Mary, God thru the Holy Ghost pressed into my spirit the following thoughts about the birth and life of Jesus as seen from Heaven:

Matthew 1: [18] *Now the birth of Jesus Christ was on this wise: When as his mother Mary was espoused to Joseph, before they came together, she was found with child of the Holy Ghost.*

For those who think I am contradicting myself when you read below that I now am calling God the father of Jesus when just above I said that the

Holy Ghost was the father of Jesus just remember that God the Father, God the Son Jesus and God the Holy Ghost are three separate entities that make up the Godhead but all three persons are one, God the Father.

Just like any father, I think God must have been very proud and excited and called out to His two archangels, Gabriel the Heavenly Messenger and Michael the Heavenly Warrior. Hey Gab hey Mikey go gather all the heavenly host and come see my baby son. Isn't He the most beautiful baby boy you have ever seen?

As time went by I believe God continued watching the young man Jesus as He was growing up and God was providing guidance and giving knowledge to Jesus as a young man growing up in the city of Nazareth.

So now we find Jesus at the age of twelve traveling to the city of Jerusalem with His parents for the Passover Feast. Instead of outside playing with the other children his age, He is sitting in the temple in Jerusalem talking and expounding the scriptures with the lawyers and religious leaders. The wisdom and knowledge of this young man blew their minds.

Many of them bewildered by His knowledge soon ask, how does this child know all these things, He's only twelve years old, what school did he attend, what Rabi taught Him these things and where did he come from?

Someone spoke up and said that Jesus came from the city of Nazareth. Another one present made the following comment: Can anything good come out of Nazareth? We all know that only the low grade of the Jewish people live in Nazareth.

Luke 2:

[42] *And when he was twelve years old, they went up to Jerusalem after the custom of the feast.*

[43] *And when they had fulfilled the days, as they returned, the child Jesus tarried behind in Jerusalem; and Joseph and his mother knew not of it.*

[44] *But they, supposing him to have been in the company, went a day's journey; and they sought him among their kinsfolk and acquaintance.*

[45] *And when they found him not, they turned back again to Jerusalem, seeking him.*

[46] *And it came to pass, that after three days they found him in the temple, sitting in the midst of the doctors, both hearing them, and asking them questions.*

[47] *And all that heard him were astonished at his understanding and answers.*

Soon Joseph, Mary, brothers, sisters and many of Jesus' acquaintances started their journey home and after a long day journeying toward Nazareth after attending the Passover Feast in Jerusalem, Jesus' earthly parents Joseph and Mary began searching for Him amongst their relatives. Not finding Him they journeyed back to Jerusalem and continued searching for Him for three days in Jerusalem. Finally His parents found Him in the temple talking to the religionist leaders and lawyers.

Joseph and Mary thought they had lost Jesus for good. They thought maybe He had been kidnapped and sold to some traders from other countries that were in town. But everything turned out good. They found Him in the temple of all places for Him to be.

When Mary his mother asked Him why He caused them so much worry, He replied with the following statement: Do you not know that I must be about My Father's business. Mary kept these saying in her heart and remembered them during the adult life of Jesus.

Jesus went home with them and submitted His life to them for the next eighteen years.

We do not hear much about the life of Jesus for the next eighteen year's except that He was subject to His earthly father and mother.

I think as a teenager Jesus probably worked with His earthly father Joseph who was a skilled carpenter by trade. Jesus was learning the carpenter trade and playing with His brothers, sisters and the other kids His age in

Nazareth. I think He ran, jumped and played the usual games that kids play.

Even though we don't have a record of the activities of Jesus during these childhood years I am sure God was having a lot of conversations with Him during these years. Jesus was getting spiritual knowledge during these years and learning obedience not only to His earthly father and mother but to God His Heavenly Father.

I'm sure God was very proud of His son during those early years watching Him every day and telling the Heavenly Host all about how Jesus was growing up and becoming such a fine young man while living on our present earth.

As our story continues we find Jesus growing up in the City of Nazareth and at the age of thirty years going to the river of Jordan and was baptized by His cousin John per the following scriptures.

Luke 3:

[21] *Now when all the people were baptized, it came to pass, that Jesus also being baptized, and praying, the heaven was opened,*

[22] *And the Holy Ghost descended in a bodily shape like a dove upon him, and a voice came from heaven, which said, Thou art my beloved Son; in thee I am well pleased.*

Have you ever wondered what the crowd of people gathered at the Jordon river that day thought when they heard this voice or noise from Heaven, I have?

Some probably thought it sounded like thunder but after looking up at the sky which was clear and blue with the sun shining brightly soon forgot all about it.

I think John must have become very excited when he saw the dove which represented the Holy Ghost descending and resting on Jesus and heard the voice of God speak very plainly as seen in the following scripture.

Luke 3: [22] *And the Holy Ghost descended in a bodily shape like a* ***dove*** *upon him, and a voice came from heaven, which said, Thou art my beloved Son; in thee I am well pleased.*

I believe John immediately knew that Jesus was the Son of God, because scripture said in:

John 3: [30] *He* ***(Jesus)*** *must increase, but I* ***(John)*** *must decrease.*

After being baptized by John scripture states that Jesus went up into the mountains to fast and pray and was tempted by Satan the devil for forty days.

Jesus finally grew tired of the temptations and speech of Satan the devil as seen in the following scripture.

Luke 4: [8], *And Jesus answered and said unto him, Get thee behind me, Satan: for it is written, Thou shalt worship the Lord thy God, and him only shalt thou serve then the devil left Him.*

During the next three years Jesus taught and expounded scriptures to His disciples and taught in all the Jewish villages and synagogues' about the soon coming Kingdom of God, healing the sick and giving repentance to all who would accept His teaching.

His physical ministry on our present earth lasted approximately three years and in the year AD30 ended at the age of thirty three.

His spiritual ministry has lasted for the last 2000 plus years and is still in effect and being effective today. It is just as fresh and exciting as when He was walking and teaching on our present earth.

Hebrews 13: [8] Says, *Jesus Christ the same yesterday, and today, and forever.*

Jesus was betrayed by one of His own disciples by the name of Judas Iscariot for thirty pieces of silver given to him by the religionist leaders from the treasury of the Jewish Temple Court for his part in the betrayal of Jesus.

Judas realizing that he had betrayed the innocent blood brought back the thirty pieces of silver to the Jewish religionist leaders and they used this money to buy a parcel of land to bury strangers in.

They had taken this money from the temple treasury to pay Judas but could not put it back into the treasury after Judas returned it because it was now classified as blood money.

Remember these were the religionist temple leaders of the Nation of Israel.

Pastor Ray Mills of the Praise and Worship Church located in Broken Arrow, Oklahoma preached a message titled Witchcraft in the Church on October 25, 2015.

He used a scripture text found in **1Samuel 15, Verse 23** which says *that rebellion is as the sin of witchcraft and stubbornness is as iniquity and idolatry.*

I believe this is what was wrong with the religionist leaders during the time that Jesus lived on our present earth. They were full of rebellion, stubbornness and idolatry which scripture says is as the sin of witchcraft.

I also believe this is what is wrong with a lot of Christians and Church Leaders in our churches today on our present earth.

We have unforgiven spirits and practice traditions which results in a rebellious spirit. We get upset at our pastor for something that he said during his sermon even though God may have been trying thru the message given by our pastor to get our attention trying to tell us something that needs to be fixed in our lives.

Sometime we come to the house of God and we are just having a bad day. Some driver cut in front of us down the street on our way to church or maybe we had a spat with our spouse and this spirit of rebellion comes upon us and we are not happy with anything or anybody and we have a bad attitude toward everyone we come into contact with.

Ladies and gentlemen this should not be and if we don't ask forgiveness quickly for these things it will fester in our spirit thus causing us to retain a rebellious spirit resulting in a witchcraft spirit in us and in our churches.

God is not prejudiced. He hates sin and loves obedience universally. He wants us to have a pure heart not a hypocritical spirit.

If you feel a rebellious spirit coming upon you, lip service repentance is of no value. You need to sincerely ask God for forgiveness and get the rebellious spirit out of your life.

James 4: [7] Says, *Submit yourselves therefore to God.* ***Resist*** *the devil, and he will flee from you.*

God is good, fair and wise and man's responsibility is to confidently place our faith in Him.

We may not always understand why God does everything that He does, but we can be assured that God loves us and that His ultimate plan's consistently includes His justice.

A life lived by faith will also be a life full of Gods' joy.

Wake up Church, God is coming for the Bride of Christ and we the Church are the Bride of Christ.

According to **Exodus 21:32** thirty pieces of silver was the price paid to the owner of a slave that had been gored by on ox belonging to another person. A sound slave was worth twice this much.

Thirty pieces of silver was the supreme insulting price paid to Judas for betraying Jesus the Messiah, God's Son, as being worth only the price of an incapacitated gored slave.

Judas not being able to live with his conscience knowing that he had betrayed the Messiah who was innocent hung himself for what he had done by betraying Jesus.

Jesus was falsely accused by false witnesses in the Roman Court of Pilate. He was sentence to death and crucified on a cross by the Romans just to appease the Jewish religionist leaders who were seeking a way to kill Him.

Matthew 27:

[**22**] *Pilate saith unto them, What shall I do then with Jesus which is called Christ? They all say unto him, Let him be crucified.*

[**23**] *And the governor said, Why, what evil hath he done? But they cried out the more, saying, Let him be crucified.*

[**24**] *When Pilate saw that he could prevail nothing, but that rather a tumult was made, he took water, and washed his hands before the multitude, saying, I am innocent of the blood of this just person: see ye to it.*

[**25**] *Then answered all the people, and said, His blood be on us, and on our children.*

God granted the Jewish people their wish in verse twenty five above that day and is still granting this same wish to the Jewish people on our present earth today.

The Jews have been persecuted and killed from that day to our present day and will be until they finally recognize and accept Jesus as their Messiah when He returns for the battle at Armageddon found in Revelation 16: 16 and Revelation Chapter 19.

It says in the following scripture to pray for the peace of Jerusalem, this includes all of us now living on this present earth.

Psalms 122: [6] *Pray for the peace of Jerusalem: they shall prosper that love thee.*

One day soon the Jewish people will realize their forefather's mistake made that day and accept Jesus as their Messiah and God will forgive them and make them a new nation which will be located on His New Earth.

As God looked down on this scene, He must have been very sorry that He ever created mankind due to mankind's treatment to His Son on our present earth.

Like any father I probably would have taken revenge on mankind immediately for the beating and death of my Son but that is not Gods' way as seen in the following scriptures.

John 3:

[**16**] *For God so loved the world, that he gave his only begotten Son, that whosoever believeth in him should not perish, but have everlasting life.*

[**17**] *For God sent not his Son into the world to condemn the world; but that the world through him might be saved.*

What a merciful God we serve.

I think Jesus as a human man living on this present earth with earthly human feelings, flesh and bone did not relish death on the cross and suffering along with the pain and agony that He went thru as seen in the following scriptures. Jesus felt the pain of the beating by the Roman soldiers, the crown of thorns driven into His head and spikes driven thru His wrist and feet and humility just like any other human being living on our present earth.

Jesus being with God in the beginning knew the plan of God for redemption for mankind so He willingly went thru the pain, agony and death on the cross so that the will and plan of His Father God for mankind might be accomplished as seen in the following scriptures.

Luke 22:

[39] *And he came out, and went, as he was wont, to the mount of Olives; and his disciples also followed him.*

[40] *And when he was at the place, he said unto them, Pray that ye enter not into temptation.*

[41] *And he was withdrawn from them about a stone's cast, and kneeled down, and prayed,*

[42] *Saying, Father, if thou be willing, remove this cup from me: nevertheless not my will, but thine, be done.*

[43] *And there appeared an angel unto him from heaven, strengthening him.*

[44] *And being in an agony he prayed more earnestly: and his sweat was as it were great drops of blood falling down to the ground.*

Oh! But this is not the end of the story, its gets better for those who accept Jesus as their Savior.

After Jesus was crucified on the cross, God sent darkness over all the earth between the sixth hour (12PM) and the ninth hour (3PM). In the ninth hour of the day Jesus said MY GOD, MY GOD, why hast thou forsaken me and gave up the ghost (died)?

The vail between the inter court and the Holy of Holies located in the Temple separated man from God. The only access man had to God for the forgiveness of sin was through the priest.

Only the priest was allowed to enter into this Holy of Holies room which represented Gods' throne room before the vail was rent by God from top to bottom.

Scripture states that the vail in the temple was rent from the top to the bottom when Jesus died. This would have been impossible for man to accomplish because of the thickness of the vail which separated man from the Holy of Holies.

God impress into my spirit that by the vail being rent from the top **which represents Gods' Throne Room in Heaven** to the bottom **which represented earth,** God was giving mankind direct access into His throne room for the forgiveness of sins thru the shed blood of Jesus. We do not need to go through a priest to ask and get forgiveness for our sins anymore, now we have direct access to God and His throne room through our Savior Jesus Christ.

Now let's look at the following scripture.

Mark 15: [**34**] *And at the ninth hour Jesus cried with a loud voice, saying, Eloi, Eloi, lama sabachthani? which is, being interpreted, My God, My God, why hast thou forsaken me?*

God had not forsaken Jesus but if He had looked down on the scene that day He would have destroyed our present earth for what mankind was doing to His Son so He just turned His head from looking at His Son for a little while. God is not a God of hate but a God of Love as seen in the following scriptures.

John 3:

[16] *For God so loved the world, that he gave his only begotten Son, that whosoever believeth in him should not perish, but have everlasting life.*

[17] *For God sent not his Son into the world to condemn the world; but that the world through him might be saved.*

[18] *He that believeth on him is not condemned: but he that believeth not is condemned already, because he hath not believed in the name of the only begotten Son of God.*

As we continue our story we see Satan overjoyed and in his excitement screaming to his cohort's telling them that soon it would be all over. Look, look Satan screamed, Jesus is dying and He is calling for God but God has forsaken Him and will not even look at Him. Jesus told everyone that He was the Son of God but even God doesn't want Him anymore.

What a party Satan and his cohorts were having in hell which had been going now for three days. Jesus is finally dead, and has been in the tomb for three days and nights. Satan declares to all his cohorts by this time He stinketh.

Satan being very excited was screaming, ranting, raving and running around flapping his arms wildly telling everyone I have won. We now have the whole earth as our domain to do whatever we want Satan screamed.

The people on this present earth will have to bow down to me now, I am in charge and I am equal to God, Satan's desire since Genesis Chapter One.

Where do you think I should set up my throne, maybe in Jerusalem? His cohorts very excited agreed while dancing around in glee.

But after three days in the tomb, God raised Jesus from the dead. The tomb could not hold Him. The earth shook and angels were seen on our present earth.

Some saints who had died previously were brought back to life and were seen walking and talking with people on this present earth.

One of Satan's demons reported to Satan that he had seen an angel roll back the stone from the mouth of the tomb.

Satan rushing to the tomb looking in screamed, it is empty, where is He, Satan screamed at his cohort's?

There was absolute chaos in hell. Satan and his cohorts are in dismay. They can't believe it, He even left His clothes. The napkin was even folded that covered His face, where did He go? They thought they had finally gotten rid of Jesus once and for all time.

Some of Satan's demon spies soon brought word to their master that they had seen Jesus alive, walking, talking and eating with his disciples on our present earth.

Satan could not believe what he was hearing, how could He do that, I thought He was dead, dead people don't eat and talk.

He was screaming, cursing and foaming at the mouth. He was stomping embers, fanning flames, and sparks were flying everywhere thru the air, how could this be.

Now there is really chaos in hell because another one of Satan's demons reported that Jesus had come to hell and had taken the keys to death and hell from the keeper of the keys sometime during the last three days that He was supposed to have been dead in the tomb.

Soon another demon reported to Satan that Jesus had removed Paradise from its location in Hades.

Satan was really mad now and screamed loosing complete control. Why was I not notified when Jesus was here, don't you have any respect for me? We could have locked Him up and melted the keys. We could have bound Him and thrown Him into the fiery pit.

Does anyone know the location where He took Paradise to?

Scripture states that during the three days that Jesus was in the earthly tomb that He descended into the lower parts of our present earth and removed those saints of old who had died believing in God from Paradise which was located in Hades to Paradise now located in Heaven awaiting the Catching up of the Church when God will bring all those who died believing in God and Jesus Christ and are asleep in Jesus back to meet the Church, the Bride of Christ in the air and they will receive their new glorified bodies along with the Church. Isn't this exciting?

Ephesians 4:

[8] *Wherefore he saith, When he ascended up on high, he led captivity captive, and gave gifts unto men.*

[9] *Now that he ascended, what is it but that he also descended first into the lower parts of the earth?*

[10] *He that descended is the same also that ascended up far above all heavens, that he might fill all things.*

Hades in the Bible before the ascension of Christ is revealed as the place of departed human spirits between death and resurrection. It was divided into two divisions, the abode of the saved and the abode of the unsaved. A great gulf separated the saved from the unsaved. The saved side was called Paradise or Abraham's bosom. The unsaved side was and is still called Hades.

Remember the story in the Bible about the beggar Lazarus whom the rich man saw in Abraham's bosom? Lazarus was in Paradise located in the center of our present earth next to Hades.

After the death of Jesus scripture say's that Jesus descended into the depths of the earth and removed Paradise and it is now located in the presence of God in Gods' Holy City in Heaven.

Ephesians 4:

[8] *Wherefore he saith, When he ascended up on high, he led captivity captive, and gave gifts unto men.*

[9] *(Now that he ascended, what is it but that he also descended first into the lower parts of the earth?*

[10] *He that descended is the same also that ascended up far above all heavens, that he might fill all things.)*

Hades after the ascension of Jesus as far as the unsaved dead are concerned, there is no location change of their place or condition revealed in scripture.

Unlike the saved the soul and spirits of the unsaved are still located in Hades or Hell awaiting the Great White Throne Judgment.

The rich man is still being tormented today just as he was in Luke Chapter 16 as seen below and will be until he is called to the Great White Thorne judgment to be judged.

At the Great White Throne Judgment, Hades will give the unsaved up and they will be judged and sentenced to spend eternity in the Lake of Fire as recorded in the following scriptures.

Revelation 20: 14 & 15.

[14] *And death and hell were cast into the lake of fire. This is the second death.*

[15] *And whosoever was not found written in the book of life was cast into the lake of fire.*

In Luke 16:19-24 we find the account of the rich man who was lost and in Hell sometimes called Hades. He was alive, conscious and in full exercise of his faculties and feelings.

[19] *There was a certain rich man, which was clothed in purple and fine linen, and fared sumptuously every day:*

[20] *And there was a certain beggar named Lazarus, which was laid at his gate, full of sores,*

[21] *And desiring to be fed with the crumbs which fell from the rich man's table: moreover the dogs came and licked his sores.*

[22] *And it came to pass, that the beggar died, and was carried by the angels into Abraham's bosom: the rich man also died, and was buried;*

[23] *And in hell he lift up his eyes, being in torments, and seeth Abraham afar off, and Lazarus in his bosom.*

[24] *And he cried and said, Father Abraham, have mercy on me, and send Lazarus, that he may dip the tip of his finger in water, and cool my tongue; for I am tormented in this flame.*

[25] *But Abraham said, Son, remember that thou in thy lifetime receivedst thy good things, and likewise Lazarus evil things: but now he is comforted, and thou art tormented.*

[26] *And beside all this, between us and you there is a great gulf fixed: so that they which would pass from hence to you cannot; neither can they pass to us, that would come from thence.*

Paradise located in heaven is a place of rest for the saved spirits of men and women who have died in Jesus and also those who died before the time of Jesus on earth that believed and served God.

Paradise is presently located in the presence of God in Heaven which is a very real place. Heaven is the abode of God, Jesus and all the heavenly host of angels.

I personally believe when a Christian dies his or her saved spirit goes to a peaceful restful place in heaven called Paradise located in the presence of God asleep in Jesus waiting for the Church to be caught up to meet God in the Air per the following scriptures.

1Thessalonians 4:

[13] *But I would not have you to be ignorant, brethren, concerning them which are asleep, that ye sorrow not, even as others which have no hope.*

[14] *For if we believe that Jesus died and rose again, even so them also which sleep in Jesus will God bring with him.*

I believe when God awakes the dead in Paradise who are asleep in Jesus he or she will not even realize they were ever dead. Time in death for the Christian is only blissful sleep and rest in Jesus and peace in the Lord in Paradise awaiting the coming back with God for the Catching up of the Church.

I think Satan and his demons were finally beginning to feel the spirit of defeat don't you? Just because Satan was defeated by Jesus when Jesus arose victorious over death and the grave he Satan has never given up on his plan to take as many men and women who could have been sons and daughters of God with him to the Lake of Fire as he can.

Don't be one of these who choose to serve Satan instead of God.

Satan was totally defeated by Jesus Christ who is alive today and is now seated on a throne at the right hand of God in Heaven's Throne Room after being resurrected from our present earth to heaven.

Ladies and gentlemen we have the privilege to live with God and Jesus for eternity when God creates His New Earth if we will only accept Jesus as our Savior and ask God for forgiveness from our sins.

God will grant us forgiveness for our sins thru the blood of His only begotten Son Jesus that was shed on the old rugged cross that whosoever believeth on Him shall not perish but have everlasting life.

Because God loved mankind so much when He looked upon the man Adam when He created him that God established His plan for redemption thru His Son Jesus Christ when sin first entered this Present Earth thru the disobedience of Adam and Eve, God continues to love you and me just as much as the day He created Adam.

During the three years that Jesus ministered on this present earth, Jesus went about doing good deeds for mankind. For example we find Jesus healing the sick, raising the dead, feeding multitudes of people and many other good deeds.

He was crucified along with two malefactors, one on each side of Him just for doing these good deeds because of the jealous attitude of the Jewish religionist temple leaders.

One of the two malefactors crucified alongside of Jesus recognizing Jesus for who He was, said to Jesus in Luke 23:42 *Lord remember me when thou comest into thy Kingdom.* This man is still at rest and asleep in Jesus in Paradise awaiting the Catching up of the Church. He will later rule and reign with Jesus on Gods' new created earth.

Jesus said to him, today you will be with me in Paradise as seen in the following scriptures.

Luke 23: 39-43:

[39] *And one of the malefactors which were hanged railed on him, saying, If thou be Christ, save thyself and us.*

[40] *But the other answering rebuked him, saying, Dost not thou fear God, seeing thou art in the same condemnation?*

[41] *And we indeed justly; for we receive the due reward of our deeds: but this man hath done nothing amiss.*

[42] *And he said unto Jesus, Lord, remember me when thou comest into thy kingdom.*

[43] *And Jesus said unto him, Verily I say unto thee, To day shalt thou be with me in paradise.*

During the three years of His ministry on our present earth Jesus selected twelve men who left all and became His disciples whom He taught concerning the soon coming Kingdom of God.

These twelve disciples were Simon Peter, James and John sons of Zebedee, Andrew, Philip, Bartholomew, Matthew, Thomas, James the son of Alphaeus, Thaddaeus, Simon the Canaanite and Judas Iscariot who betrayed Jesus.

One of these twelve men, Judas Iscariot who loved money more than God, who was the treasurer for Jesus and His disciples gave up his salvation and chose to serve and follow Satan by accepting thirty pieces of silver from the religionist temple leaders of that day by betraying Jesus. After realizing what he had done he gave back the 30 pieces of silver and committed suicide by hanging himself.

Judas has regretted that decision to betray Jesus every second, minute, hour, day, month, year since that day and will regret it thru out eternity in the Lake of Fire, never to forget.

Can you imagine how Judas feels at this very moment that you are reading this book knowing that he could be in the presents of God, asleep in Jesus resting in Paradise along with the other eleven disciples that he traveled with for three years during the ministry of Jesus awaiting the Catching up of the Church. Judas is currently tormented in Hell and later will be cast into the Lake of Fire for eternity.

The reward for sin is spending eternity in the Lake of Fire. Don't go there.

Another one of His disciples by the name of Peter denied knowing Jesus three times while Jesus was being interrogated by the religionist leaders in the temple court after Judas betrayed Jesus.

Peter later repented and was forgiven. He became one of the great leaders in the early Church.

We find in **John 21:15-16-17** Jesus cooking by the sea shore after He had risen from the dead and eating with some of the disciples including Peter who had denied Him. Jesus asked Peter if he loved Him three times.

Since Peter had denied knowing Jesus three times on the night of His arrest by the religionist leaders, maybe Jesus was testing Peter by asking him if he loved Him these three times.

Peter said in **John 21 verse seventeen**, *Lord thou knowest all things, thou knowest that I love thee. Jesus said to Peter feed my sheep.*

I think Peter finally got the message Jesus was giving to him and devoted the rest of his life in ministry to the Jewish people expounding to them the message that Jesus Christ was indeed the Messiah that they had been looking for.

This just shows how much God and Jesus love's us. They are willing to forgive us when we fall if we will only ask them for forgiveness. If you have not done this please do it now, tomorrow may be too late.

After Jesus ascended back to Heaven and was seated at the right hand of Father God a replacement for Judas Iscariot was selected, a man by the name of Matthias.

These twelve disciples became the fathers and forerunners of the Church today which make up The Bride of Christ.

After the death and resurrection of Jesus, the Church was born into existence and it has now been a little over two thousand years since His death and His affect upon mankind is still real today just as it was during His ministry while living and walking upon our present earth.

Soon the 70th week of Daniel's End Time Vision known as the Seven Year Tribulation Period will begin.

Soon God will judge this present earth for the last time before creating the New Earth as recorded in the 21st Chapter of the book of Revelation.

Gods' Church is still alive and souls are being born into and added to the Kingdom of God each and every day to the dismay of Satan.

Luke 24:

[45] *Then opened he their understanding, that they might understand the scriptures,*

[46] *And said unto them, Thus it is written, and thus it behoved Christ to suffer, and to rise from the dead the third day:*

[47] *And that repentance and remission of sins should be preached in his name among all nations, beginning at Jerusalem.*

[48] *And ye are witnesses of these things.*

[49] *And, behold, I send the promise of my Father upon you: but tarry ye in the city of Jerusalem, until ye be endued with power from on high.*

[50] *And he led them out as far as to Bethany, and he lifted up his hands, and blessed them.*

[51] *And it came to pass, while he blessed them, he was parted from them, and carried up into heaven.*

[52] *And they worshipped him, and returned to Jerusalem with great joy:*

[53] *And were continually in the temple, praising and blessing God. Amen.*

As we read in the scriptures just before Jesus was received up into Heaven that He gave instructions to His disciples to go back to Jerusalem and wait for the enduing power of the Holy Ghost which He would ask His Father God to send to them, which Father God did.

As we continue our journey on our present earth we find another interesting man found in the scriptures of the New Testament by the name of Saul.

This man was probably the most dreaded and feared of all men during the early time of the Church. Saul persecuted the Church constantly and he put many Christians in prison and caused the death of many.

He personally had the permission of the religionist leader's to hunt down Christians to either kill them or throw them into prison.

As we continue our journey on this present earth, scripture states that one day Saul was traveling on the road to Damascus with orders to search out and arrest Christian's when he had an encounter with Jesus Christ Himself.

This encounter with Jesus is found in the following scriptures.

Acts 9:

[1] *And Saul, yet breathing out threatenings and slaughter against the disciples of the Lord, went unto the high priest,*

[2] *And desired of him letters to Damascus to the synagogues, that if he found any of this way, whether they were men or women, he might bring them bound unto Jerusalem.*

[3] *And as he journeyed, he came near Damascus: and suddenly there shined round about him a light from heaven:*

[4] *And he fell to the earth, and heard a voice saying unto him, Saul, Saul, why persecutest thou me?*

[5] *And he said, Who art thou, Lord? And the Lord said, I am Jesus whom thou persecutest: it is hard for thee to kick against the pricks.*

Saul received a complete make over that day. From that time on he became one of the strongest believers and ministers of Christianity during the early time of the Church on our present earth.

It is thru the preaching and teaching of Saul whose name was changed to Paul in the book of Acts Chapter Thirteen that we Gentiles can now enjoy the saving grace of God and our Christianity today.

Paul was the author who wrote most of the New Testament Books found in the Bible.

Scripture states that thru the persecution of the early Church that the Church grew mightily and many souls were added to the Church daily.

This is why I believe that the Church now living on our present earth will go thru the first three and one half years of the Seven Year Tribulation Period. The Church of today is full of spots and wrinkles. God said that he would spew out of his mouth Christians and Churches that conform to the ways of this world on this present earth instead of Gods' ways.

Ladies and gentlemen we need to get ready for the coming of God for the Church and stop playing church trying to appease the world and get serious about serving God.

There are many other great men mentioned in the New Testament who God used to further the gospel of Jesus Christ. I just don't have room in this book to write about them all.

I encourage you to read God's Word and get acquainted with all those men and women written about in the Bible. They were real people living on a real earth, serving a real God.

Are you willing to be used by God to further the gospel on this present earth today?

As we live our lives in today's society it may seem that the Church is losing ground to Satan and his forces but let me assure you that God is still in control and soon God will come to catch up a Church that is without spot or wrinkle who will be the Bride for His Son Jesus Christ who sacrificed His life for us.

We live on this present earth today with men and women whose main desire is to make this earth that was created by God into a manmade social society having a one world government and a one world religion not associated with God.

Man is teaching that we will in time evolve into a perfect race of people and our lives on our present earth will only get better under the rule of one government and one religion.

This false teaching is called evolution by mankind in today's society. Ladies and gentlemen we did not evolve from an ape or monkey as some teach.

Ladies and gentlemen we are the descendants of Adam a man who was created by God in Gods' own image as recorded in the book of Genesis. Gods' image is talking about the spiritual man not what the mortal man looks like.

This makes you and I a person created in Gods' own image also. Praise God.

If you believe in the theory of evolution than you must believe that God does not exist and if He does the Bible is not telling the truth about God creating man in His own image found in the book of Genesis of our Bible.

Lying also would break one of the ten commandments of God given to Moses on Mount Sinai so I choose to believe God not man.

I believe the theory of evolution was created by Satan and those who teach and believe this theory are the servants and followers of Satan.

As we listen to news reports we hear of killings, robberies, rape and many other crimes committed against society on Our Present Earth constantly every day.

This does not sound like we are evolving into a better society to me, don't you agree?

Satan is trying very hard to take as many people to hell with him as he can. Not just because he hates people but because he hates God and His Son Jesus who offers hope for the future of mankind to live in eternal bliss on the New Earth to come.

Satan already knows what his eternal future holds for him. He knows that he will be cast into the Lake of Fire with all unbelievers for eternity.

I believe one of the reasons it is so difficult to convince unbelievers to accept Jesus as their Savior on our present earth today is because mankind with the help of Satan has made movies and stories of Heaven and Hell seem like fantasy stories or somewhat of a fairy tale instead of teaching Heaven and Hell as very real places.

Many preach and teach in vague messages about mankind's financial prosperity not really teaching unbelievers the real truth about Heaven and Hell not wanting to scare or hurt people's feelings while trying to make people feel good about how they live.

A lot of ministers while preaching relate stories about how God has prospered them financially and their whole message is telling stories about how God has blessed them financially and that God will bless you financially if you sow a seed by sending them money. This not only is done by Ministers on TV but in our churches as well.

I appreciate the work they do to further the Gospel of God on this present earth and the financial blessing that God has given them but what about preaching the message of salvation and explaining about the wonders that believers are going to enjoy living with God and Jesus on the New Earth and also about the torments of Hell and the Lake of Fire which unbelievers will get to enjoy with Satan for eternity.

I don't know about you but I can't remember hearing a message explaining to me about the wonders of what Christians will be experiencing while living on the New Earth.

Many Ministers and Christians don't believe that God is going to create a New Earth for the Church to rule and reign on with Jesus even though Gods' Holy Word says this is going to happen. Most teach that we are going to live in heaven for eternity.

Also it has been a long time since I heard a message discribing the torments that unbelievers will be experiencing in the Lake of Fire as seen in the following scriptures.

Rev.20: [10] *And the devil that deceived them was cast into the lake of* ***fire and brimstone****, where the beast and the false prophet are, and shall be tormented day and night for ever and ever.*

Rev.21: [8] *But the fearful, and unbelieving, and the abominable, and murderers, and whoremongers, and sorcerers, and idolaters, and all liars, shall have their part in the lake which burneth with* ***fire and brimstone****: which is the second death.*

I remember in my early years hearing the phrase that ministers preached hell so hot and real that you could almost feel the flames. From these messages many men and women made the decision to accept God and His salvation by accepted Jesus as their Savior and they lived for God and the Church grew. What has happened to this message?

Today is seems that the messages we hear are all about reaching higher levels and achieving financial prosperity in serving God not about Heaven or Hell.

Don't get me wrong I believe if we live godly lives God will not only prosper us spiritually but financially also. I just cannot find scripture's in our Bible which describe different levels in serving God. Maybe I have just overlooked these or I am not smart enough to recognize these scriptures. I don't believe the thief on the cross next to Jesus who asked Jesus to remember him when Jesus established Gods' Kingdom had time to search for different levels, he only wanted forgiveness and God forgave him to receive eternal life to live on the new earth just as He will do for you and me.

The only different positions I find in scripture are found in the following verse and these don't sound like different levels but spiritual gifts that should be prevalent in our churches.

These are not the same gifts as the fruit of the spirit found in Galatians Chapter 5, verses 22 and 23.

This is talking about available spiritual gifts that should be prevalent and working in our Churches on our present earth today and how God will use us in these different positions in life and equip us to be able to teach and serve others by doing His will while serving Him on this present earth as seen in the following scriptures.

Ephesians 4: [8] *Wherefore he saith, When he ascended up on high, he led captivity captive, and gave gifts unto men.*

Ephesians 4 [11] *And he gave some, apostles; and some, prophets; and some, evangelists; and some, pastors and teachers.*

These are spiritual gifts made available to mankind given by Jesus to men and women when He ascended up on high into Heaven and these gifts are to be used for the perfecting of the saints for the work of the ministry to edify the body of Christ in the Church found in verse twelve.

Ephesians 4: [12] *For the perfecting of the saints, for the work of the ministry, for the edifying of the body of Christ:*

It seems in today's Christian circles that everyone wants to be a prophet or an apostle and they are always giving someone a word of knowledge. When I listen to some of these self-proclaimed prophets and apostles prophecy, it is mostly about mankind receiving monetary or material gain not spiritual words of knowledge which would edify in the building up of mankind's faith spiritually. I am not saying that true prophets or apostles don't exists but I am speaking about many self-proclaimed prophets and apostles who are speaking words just to make mankind believe they are very spiritual while trying to proclaim themselves as someone special.

True prophets or apostles prophesy the correct message given by God for edification to those prophesied to.

I believe the gifts found in the above scripture verse eleven are speaking about spiritual blessings for the edifying of the Church as explained in verse twelve. I have even heard some self-proclaimed prophets tell people that they are called into the ministry when most of the time God has not spoken to this person concerning being called into the ministry at all. They soon fail and many even stop serving God.

I believe God is capable of letting us know personally His will for our lives Himself instead of going thru some man or woman who is trying to promote themselves as a prophet or an apostle of God to further their own agenda.

Forgive me if you think I am being critical but the prophets that I read about in the Bible were judging the sins of the people to bring them back to repentance to God not speaking about mankind receiving monetary gain like some are doing today.

I personally believe that those giving a word of knowledge or a prophetic word to an individual in a church service should not grab a microphone or speak so loudly that the whole congregation can hear. The whole congregation does not need to know everything concerning the need of those being given a word of knowledge to.

I do believe in prophets, apostles, evangelists, pastors and teachers but I think their ministry is for the edifying of the Church the body of Christ but many have taken these positions to the extreme to build themselves up as someone special.

Scripture says in 1John 4: [1] *Beloved, believe not every spirit, but try the spirits whether they are of God: because many false prophets are gone out into the world.*

In this book we are studying about the future of men and women's lives and where they will spend eternity. I think this should be the message not only of ministers but we laymen also, don't you?

I believe the real message of Jesus Christ and God is about the forgiveness of sin and where mankind is going to spend eternity which is for ever and ever.

We will either live in eternal bliss with Jesus, God and all other believers on Gods' New Earth or with Satan and his followers in a place called in the Bible the Lake of Fire where the torments for those who are banished there are very real and will never cease but will last for eternity.

Most Christians if asked cannot explain to unbelievers what people will be doing or enjoying for eternity because most don't know themselves and they just say something like, we will spend eternity praising God and Jesus in Heaven, visiting with friends and family while living in a mansion and that Hell is going to be a very hot place so don't go there.

If you were an unbeliever would the above explanation make you want to become a Christian believer? I think not.

I have ask Christians who think that we are going to live in Heaven for eternity what they think living in Heaven will be like and some have told me that living in Heaven was going to be so much better than the life they have lived here on our present earth and that is a good enough for them. In other words they did not know, sorry that explanation is not good enough for me.

I am the type of person who likes details and Gods' Word gives detail information if we will only read and study it. It says that we will be kings and priest on Gods' New Earth while ruling and reigning with Jesus. Maybe this is why God spoke into my spirit thru the Holy Ghost to write His message to the world we are living in today in this book. I am not a minister with a pulpit to preach from so I guess this book becomes my pulpit.

Ladies and gentlemen Heaven and Hell are very real places. Heaven is where the Throne Room of God is presently located but it will soon be re-located to the New Earth that God is going to create for Christians to live on and Hell or Hades is where unbelievers currently await the Great White Throne Judgment where they will be judged and then cast alive into the Lake of Fire to be tormented for eternity along with Satan, the antichrist and the false prophet, fallen angels, demons and all other unbelievers. This is called in scripture the second death.

Ladies and gentlemen I can assure you that the Lake of Fire will not be a cool place to spend eternity.

We need to study God's Word so that we can relate to those who are unsaved the truth concerning living with God and Jesus for eternity on

Gods' New Earth or living with Satan and his cohorts in torment in the Lake of Fire for eternity.

This present earth will soon erupt into World War III described in the book of Revelation in God's Holy Word as the Seven Year Tribulation Period, also known as the 70th week of Daniel's End Time Vision found in Daniel Chapter 9, verse 24 concerning our present earth.

The Seven Year Tribulation Period will be the worst time for mankind ever recorded in history on this present earth.

It will escalate with the last three and one half years of God's wrath being poured out as judgment on sinful men and women for not accepting Jesus the Son of God as their Savior.

God will judge sinful mankind at the Great White Throne Judgment and they will be doomed to live for eternity in the Lake of Fire along with Lucifer who is Satan the devil, the antichrist, the false prophet, demons, the fallen angels and all men and women who chose to follow Satan instead of God.

The leaders of the nations on our present earth are presently searching for answers to this earth's problems but cannot find the answers because they are trusting in the knowledge of man instead of trusting in God.

The nations on this present earth are ready and will accept a world leader who promises to solve all their political and financial problems and who will later become a leader described in the Bible as the antichrist.

He will become the leader of Ten Middle Eastern Nations which represents the revived Roman Empire that make up the first beast (Satan's) empire found in Revelation Chapter 13. He will be the counterfeit of the true Christ.

Though it may seem that true believers have been lost in the millions of unbelievers, God has not lost sight of each and every one of us, and like

Daniel, He will bring us through whatever troubles or temptations that comes into our lives, if we will only put our trust in Him.

If we commit our ways to God, He will guide and bless our walk thru life on this present earth.

To the carnal man it must seem like there is little hope for mankind on our present earth. That is why death by suicide is so high but Gods' Word says there is hope and the Bible makes it clear that there will come a time of world peace and happiness for mankind on the New Earth for those who have accepted Jesus as their Savior.

Mankind is searching diligently for happiness and peace on this present earth today but cannot achieve it, why, because mankind puts their trust in man. Mankind does not seek or ask God for His wisdom for their lives.

Many nations and people long for peace and sometimes fight wars for it. Peace treaties between nations are negotiated for peace but most treaties are soon broken. Yet peace remains more elusive than ever. We hear of wars and rumors of wars between nations and people all over our present earth every day in the news.

I believe we are in the beginning stages of sorrows which will lead us to the beginning of the Seven Year Tribulation Period known as Daniel's 70th week of his End Time Vision.

Matthew 24:14 says: *And this gospel of the kingdom shall be preached in all the world for a witness unto all nations; and then shall the end come.*

A lot of people quote and read this scripture with the thought that the end of time for our present earth cannot come soon because the gospel has not been preached to all people in the entire world.

The above verse says the gospel of the kingdom shall be preached **in all the world** for a witness unto **All Nations** not people. Because of modern day technology I doubt if there is a nation left on this present earth that the gospel has not been heard or preached in.

This Gospel of the Kingdom shall be preached in all the world for a witness unto all nations, **and then shall the end come**.

Are we preaching and teaching this Gospel of the Kingdom? This does not say that the Gospel of the Kingdom has to be preached to all the people of the world, just preached for a witness unto all nations, **not all of the people in all nations** as some believe which is just another tactic of the devil to deceive people into believing they have plenty of time thinking that all the people on our present earth have not heard the gospel.

The Bible says that peace will come and soon but only thru God.

The fulfillment of Bible prophecy concerning the end of this present earth is rapidly appearing. We cannot stop these prophetic events from taking place because they are on God's timetable not ours.

God will not and does not change His plans. These prophetic events will usher in the coming of God for the church and then the return of Jesus Christ the Son of God to establish His Father Gods' earthly Kingdom to be located on this present earth at the beginning of the One Thousand Year Millennium and then He will turn this Kingdom over to Father God when God creates the New Earth at the end of the One Thousand Year Millennium as seen in the following scripture.

1 Corinthians 15: 24: *Then cometh the end, when he shall have delivered up the kingdom to God, even the Father; when he shall have put down all rule and all authority and power.*

The above verse does away with the teaching of many Christians that we will be living in Heaven for eternity instead of on Gods' new created earth, doesn't it.

This earthly kingdom will last for eternity on God's New Created Earth.

Are you ready to meet Christ? If not, now is the time to get ready.

Just remember that the Church belongs to a kingdom that is not of this world at this present time but it will belong to a earthly kingdom known as the Kingdom of God that will be established on the New Earth with the Holy City New Jerusalem as its capitol located in the Nation of Israel after the One Thousand Year Millennium.

Believers will get to enjoy the power of the Catching up of the Church, the Marriage Supper of the Lamb and the promise of Jesus to all who believe as seen in the following scriptures.

1Thessalonians 4:

[**13**] *But I would not have you to be ignorant, brethren, concerning them which are asleep, that ye sorrow not, even as others which have no hope.*

[**14**] *For if we believe that Jesus died and rose again, even so them also which* ***sleep in Jesus*** *will* **GOD** ***bring with him.***

Who is bringing them that sleep in Jesus to meet the Saints in the Catching up of the Church, this scripture fourteen above says it will be **GOD HIMSELF** not Jesus.

We have been taught that Jesus is coming back for the Church but this scripture says that it is **GOD HIMSELF** who is coming for the Church.

Ladies and gentlemen we need to read and comprehend what the scriptures are really saying to us. Don't take man's word, take Gods' Word.

[15] *For this we say unto you by the word of the Lord, that we which are alive and remain unto the coming of the Lord shall not prevent them which are asleep.*

[16] *For the Lord himself* ***(GOD)*** *shall descend from heaven with a shout, with the voice of the archangel* ***(Gabriel),*** *and with the trump of God: and the dead in Christ shall rise first:*

[17] *Then we which are alive and remain shall be caught up together with them in the clouds, to meet the Lord in the air: and so shall we ever be with the Lord.*

[18] *Wherefore comfort one another with these words.*

These scriptures says that it will be God who will bring those resting in Paradise who are asleep in Jesus back with Him to meet the Church in the Air for all to receive their glorified bodies and then He will present the Church the Bride to His Son Jesus.

As an example let's discuss the subject of marriage on our present earth today. The bridegroom doesn't come to the bride's residence to receive or transport his bride to the location for the wedding ceremony. The bride is brought to the church or to the place for the marriage ceremony by her father or someone who represents her father if he is not available who presents her to the bridegroom.

It will be the same in the Catching up of the Church who is the Bride of Christ. Father God will come and receive the Church the Bride of Christ to present her to His Son Jesus who is the bridegroom as seen in the above scriptures.

Father God is the father of the Church the Bride. Jesus is the bridegroom.

Praise God for His Son Jesus and God's plan of redemption. We thank you Jesus for redeeming us from a world of sin thru your death on the cross.

As previously stated, God's plan for mankind's redemption was thru the death of His Son Jesus Christ. This plan was established from the time sin first entered the world thru the deceit of Adam and Eve by Satan in the Garden of Eden.

God is still looking down upon our present earth from the balcony of Heaven and looking at each and every one who has accepted His Son Jesus as their Savior and is very proud to call you His son or His daughter.

Live your life today for Jesus because if you wait tomorrow may be too late.

If you have not accepted Jesus as your Savior please do so today and get prepared to live with God, Jesus and all the men and women who have accepted Jesus as their Savior on Gods' new created earth.

By accepting Jesus as your Savior you will have the privilege of living on Gods' New Earth that we will be discussing more in the next chapters.

CHAPTER TWO

TOPICS OF THE BIBLE

In this chapter we will be discussing the following topics, Jesus-mankind-visions-measurement of time-the one thousand year millennium-the seven year tribulation period-the division of land for the twelve tribes of Israel on the New Earth-traditional teachings-the Church Bride and nations located on the New Earth.

Ladies and Gentlemen it's time we face some cold hard facts:

Mankind has two options:

First option, mankind can either accept that there is an Almighty God who is about to come and receive the Church as the Bride to marry His Son Jesus and then later God will send Jesus back to our present earth to battle Satan and his armies at the battle at Armageddon. After these armies are destroyed Jesus will set up Father Gods' earthly Kingdom on our present earth at the beginning of the One Thousand Year Millennium.

Jesus will then rule over all nations on this present earth with the armies of Heaven who will enforce His rules and leadership so that there will be peace and harmony when God creates the New Earth where Gods' Kingdom will be located at the end of the One Thousand Year Millennium as the Bible teaches.

Second option, mankind can keep on serving Satan and fighting each other until all human life on our present earth will be destroyed but mankind will still have to face eternity either to live on Gods' new earth or live in the Lake of Fire with Satan and his followers.

We hear a lot today about the separation of church and state in today's society. God never intended it to be this way.

In Gods' government on the New Earth the church and governments of all nations will work together in perfect harmony without challenges as to whether the government should or should not intrude into religion or religion into government.

All infighting amongst government officials will end. No more democrats, independent, republicans, tea party or any other political party.

There will only be one governing party and that will be God's. There will be absolute unity in every aspect of Gods' government.

Our present earth has been somewhat limited from Gods' physical presence since Adam and Eve was deceived by Satan in the Garden of Eden and God expelled them from the Garden of Eden.

God has shown Himself a few times to men like Abraham, Samuel and some others on this present earth as recorded in the Bible but not very often. He now uses the Holy Ghost as His ambassador to mankind on our present earth.

I have heard and read stories about God, Jesus or an angel paying a personal visit to men and women during our present time on our present earth but as previous discussed I find only one time in the bible that Jesus paid a personal visit to anyone on this present earth after ascending to His throne in Heaven and that was when He visited Saul on the road to Damascus found in the following scriptures.

Acts 9:

[1] *And Saul, yet breathing out threatenings and slaughter against the disciples of the Lord, went unto the high priest,*

[2] *And desired of him letters to Damascus to the synagogues, that if he found any of this way, whether they were men or women, he might bring them bound unto Jerusalem.*

[3] *And as he journeyed, he came near Damascus: and suddenly there shined round about him a light from heaven:*

[4] *And he fell to the earth, and heard a voice saying unto him, Saul, Saul, why persecutest thou me?*

[5] *And he said, Who art thou, Lord? And the Lord said, I am Jesus whom thou persecutest: it is hard for thee to kick against the pricks.*

I believe God or Jesus could physically come back to our present earth for a visit anytime they so desire because of the following scripture found in:

Matthew 19: [26] *But Jesus beheld them, and said unto them, With men this is impossible; but with God all things are possible.*

To my knowledge I personally have never experienced a live visit from God, Jesus or an angel on our present earth that I know of. I might have been visited by an angel and not known it per the following scripture found in Hebrews Chapter Thirteen below.

Hebrews 13: [2] *Be not forgetful to entertain strangers: for thereby some have entertained angels unawares.*

The physical presence of God and Jesus with us will be possible for all believers on the New Created Earth where the personal presence of God and Jesus will be available for everyone to enjoy every day on the New Earth.

God loved mankind so much that He sent His Son Jesus to die for our sins so that we could become Gods' sons' and daughters' born into His God Family.

After Jesus ascended back into Heaven He ask Father God to send the Holy Ghost the third entity of the Trinity Godhead to be our Teacher, Comforter and Guide in this life, which God did.

Have you accepted Jesus as your Savior and received the Holy Ghost as your Teacher, Comforter and Guide?

If not please do so today, tomorrow may be too late.

2 Peter 3:9 states: *The Lord is not slack concerning His promises, but is longsuffering to us-ward, not willing that any should perish, but that all should come to repentance.*

Gods' desire is for everyone to be saved and to live with Him, Jesus and all other Saints on the New Earth for eternity. God will not force anyone to serve Him and has given each of us the ability to make a personal choice as to whom we will serve, God or Satan.

If we love God, we will have a love and compassion for others just like God and Jesus does.

You have a choice today to either choose God and become a citizen in Gods' Kingdom on the New Earth or choose Satan and become a citizen of hell and live in the Lake of Fire for eternity.

You ***have already*** made this choose. Think about it, which one did you make?

Eternity has a beginning but no ending. Eternity starts with man's last breath but there is no end to eternity. How close are we to eternity, only one breath away, think about it as you breathe your next breath?

Mankind has been deceived and believed the lies of Satan for almost six thousand years.

I believe Gods' original plan for redemption for all mankind covered a period of seven thousand years. We are about to reach the finish of six thousand years of Gods' plan and the beginning of the last one thousand years.

I submit my thoughts as to the breakdown for these years: Six thousand years for earthly man's form of government and one thousand years for the reign of Jesus during the One Thousand Year Millennium broken down per the following:

Four thousand years from Adam to the death of Jesus Christ the Son of God when he was crucified on the cross and then two thousand years since Jesus rose from the dead until the end of the seven year tribulation period, then one thousand years for the Millennium reign of Jesus when Jesus will come back to our present earth with the armies of Heaven for the battle at Armageddon. He then will set up the Kingdom of God on our present earth for the One Thousand Year Millennium.

Jesus will sit on the throne of David in Jerusalem during the One Thousand Year Millennium after establishing the Kingdom of God ruling over all nations on our present earth for one thousand years getting believers ready to live on Gods' New Earth for eternity and the unbeliever to be judged at the Great White Throne Judgment to be cast alive into the Lake of Fire to live for eternity.

Per the measurements of man this is a total of seven thousand years.

The two thousand years since the death of Jesus has been extended for the period of Grace that we will discuss below. How long will this period of Grace last, only God knows? God does not measure time as man does.

Let's look in the book of Daniel concerning the Nation of Israel.

In Daniel 9: [2] *In the first year of his reign I Daniel understood by books the number of the years, whereof the word of the LORD* ***(God)*** *came to Jeremiah the prophet, that he would accomplish seventy years in the desolations of Jerusalem.*

The above verse is speaking about the 70 years that Daniel and the other Israeli POW's would experience after they were taken captive and brought to Babylon by King Nebuchadnezzar after he captured Israel. Bible history states that this was probably in the year of 605 BC.

Israel was to be in captivity for 70 years as punishment for the transgressions of God's Holy Sabbaths per the writings of the prophet Jeremiah. Sin was committed by the Israeli leaders and the Israeli people by not trusting and serving God as God had instructed in the law given to Moses.

Don't confuse these seventy years with the seventy weeks of Daniels End Time Vision for the finishing of Israel's transgression as written in Daniel Chapter 9, they are not the same.

King Cyrus of the Medes and Persians Empire wrote a decree giving permission so that some of the Israeli POW's could journey back to Jerusalem for the Jewish Second Temple to be rebuilt and He even provided supplies for the rebuilding of the temple. Per Bible history the probably year for this was 539 BC. For some reason this was delayed and never came to pass.

This was for the rebuilding of the Second Temple only, not the rebuilding of the City of Jerusalem.

This is also written in the book of Ezra Chapter 1, let's look at these scriptures.

Ezra 1: First decree by Cyrus King of Persia giving permission to rebuild the Second Temple in Jerusalem (539 BC).

[1] *Now in the first year of Cyrus king of Persia, that the word of the LORD by the mouth of Jeremiah might be fulfilled, the LORD stirred up the spirit of Cyrus king of Persia, that he made a proclamation throughout all his kingdom, and put it also in writing, saying,*

[2] *Thus saith Cyrus king of Persia, The LORD God of heaven hath given me all the kingdoms of the earth; and he hath charged me to build him an house at Jerusalem, which is in Judah.*

[3] *Who is there among you of all his people? his God be with him, and let him go up to Jerusalem, which is in Judah, and build the house of the LORD God of Israel, (he is the God,) which is in Jerusalem.*

[4] *And whosoever remaineth in any place where he sojourneth, let the men of his place help him with silver, and with gold, and with goods, and with beasts, beside the freewill offering for the house of God that is in Jerusalem.*

[5] *Then rose up the chief of the fathers of Judah and Benjamin, and the priests, and the Levites, with all them whose spirit God had raised, to go up to build the house of the LORD which is in Jerusalem.*

[6] *And all they that were about them strengthened their hands with vessels of silver, with gold, with goods, and with beasts, and with precious things, beside all that was willingly offered.*

[7] *Also Cyrus the king brought forth the vessels of the house of the LORD, which Nebuchadnezzar had brought forth out of Jerusalem, and had put them in the house of his gods;*

[8] *Even those did Cyrus king of Persia bring forth by the hand of Mithredath the treasurer, and numbered them unto Sheshbazzar, the prince of Judah.*

[9] *And this is the number of them: thirty chargers of gold, a thousand chargers of silver, nine and twenty knives,*

[10] *Thirty basons of gold, silver basons of a second sort four hundred and ten, and other vessels a thousand.*

[11] *All the vessels of gold and of silver were five thousand and four hundred. All these did Sheshbazzar bring up with them of the captivity that were brought up from Babylon unto Jerusalem.*

The Jews again appealed to King Darius king of Persia to let them go and rebuild the Second Temple and reminded him of the decree made by King Cyrus in 539 BC found in the following scriptures.

Ezra 6: Second decree (Bible history years 519/518 BC) given by Darius King of Persia giving permission for the rebuilding of the Second Temple in Jerusalem.

[1] *Then Darius the king made a decree, and search was made in the house of the rolls, where the treasures were laid up in Babylon.*

[2] *And there was found at Achmetha, in the palace that is in the province of the Medes, a roll, and therein was a record thus written:*

[3] *In the first year of Cyrus the king the same Cyrus the king made a decree concerning the house of God at Jerusalem, Let the house be builded, the place where they offered sacrifices, and let the foundations thereof be strongly laid; the height thereof threescore cubits, and the breadth thereof threescore cubits;*

[4] *With three rows of great stones, and a row of new timber: and let the expences be given out of the king's house:*

[5] *And also let the golden and silver vessels of the house of God, which Nebuchadnezzar took forth out of the temple which is at Jerusalem, and brought unto Babylon, be restored, and brought again unto the temple which is at Jerusalem, every one to his place, and place them in the house of God.*

[6] *Now therefore, Tatnai, governor beyond the river, Shethar-boznai, and your companions the Apharsachites, which are beyond the river, be ye far from thence:*

[7] *Let the work of this house of God alone; let the governor of the Jews and the elders of the Jews build this house of God in his place.*

[8] *Moreover I make a decree what ye shall do to the elders of these Jews for the building of this house of God: that of the king's goods, even of the tribute beyond the river, forthwith expences be given unto these men, that they be not hindered.*

[9] *And that which they have need of, both young bullocks, and rams, and lambs, for the burnt offerings of the God of heaven, wheat, salt, wine, and oil, according to the appointment of the priests which are at Jerusalem, let it be given them day by day without fail:*

[10] *That they may offer sacrifices of sweet savours unto the God of heaven, and pray for the life of the king, and of his sons.*

[11] *Also I have made a decree, that whosoever shall alter this word, let timber be pulled down from his house, and being set up, let him be hanged thereon; and let his house be made a dunghill for this.*

[12] *And the God that hath caused his name to dwell there destroy all kings and people, that shall put to their hand to alter and to destroy this house of God which is at Jerusalem. I Darius have made a decree; let it be done with speed.*

Again for some reason this trip was delayed the second time and never happened.

Ezra 7: Third decree given by Artaxerxes King of Persia again giving permission to Ezra for the rebuilding of the Second Temple in Jerusalem (Bible history year of 458 BC).

[11] *Now this is the copy of the letter that the king Artaxerxes gave unto Ezra the priest, the scribe, even a scribe of the words of the commandments of the LORD, and of his statutes to Israel.*

[12] *Artaxerxes, king of kings, unto Ezra the priest, a scribe of the law of the God of heaven, perfect peace, and at such a time.*

[13] *I make a decree, that all they of the people of Israel, and of his priests and Levites, in my realm, which are minded of their own freewill to go up to Jerusalem, go with thee.*

[14] *Forasmuch as thou art sent of the king, and of his seven counsellers, to inquire concerning Judah and Jerusalem, according to the law of thy God which is in thine hand;*

[15] *And to carry the silver and gold, which the king and his counsellers have freely offered unto the God of Israel, whose habitation is in Jerusalem,*

[16] *And all the silver and gold that thou canst find in all the province of Babylon, with the freewill offering of the people, and of the priests, offering willingly for the house of their God which is in Jerusalem:*

[17] *That thou mayest buy speedily with this money bullocks, rams, lambs, with their meat offerings and their drink offerings, and offer them upon the altar of the house of your God which is in Jerusalem.*

[18] *And whatsoever shall seem good to thee, and to thy brethren, to do with the rest of the silver and the gold, that do after the will of your God.*

[19] *The vessels also that are given thee for the service of the house of thy God, those deliver thou before the God of Jerusalem.*

[20] *And whatsoever more shall be needful for the house of thy God, which thou shalt have occasion to bestow, bestow it out of the king's treasure house.*

[21] *And I, even I Artaxerxes the king, do make a decree to all the treasurers which are beyond the river, that whatsoever Ezra the priest, the scribe of the law of the God of heaven, shall require of you, it be done speedily,*

[22] *Unto an hundred talents of silver, and to an hundred measures of wheat, and to an hundred baths of wine, and to an hundred baths of oil, and salt without prescribing how much.*

[23] *Whatsoever is commanded by the God of heaven, let it be diligently done for the house of the God of heaven: for why should there be wrath against the realm of the king and his sons?*

[24] *Also we certify you, that touching any of the priests and Levites, singers, porters, Nethinims, or ministers of this house of God, it shall not be lawful to impose toll, tribute, or custom, upon them.*

[25] *And thou, Ezra, after the wisdom of thy God, that is in thine hand, set magistrates and judges, which may judge all the people that are beyond the river, all such as know the laws of thy God; and teach ye them that know them not.*

[26] *And whosoever will not do the law of thy God, and the law of the king, let judgment be executed speedily upon him, whether it be unto death, or to banishment, or to confiscation of goods, or to imprisonment.*

[27] *Blessed be the LORD God of our fathers, which hath put such a thing as this in the king's heart, to beautify the house of the LORD which is in Jerusalem:*

[28] *And hath extended mercy unto me before the king, and his counsellers, and before all the king's mighty princes. And I was strengthened as the hand of the LORD my God was upon me, and I gathered together out of Israel chief men to go up with me.*

The exact date that Ezra traveled to Jerusalem for the rebuilding of the Temple is not stated in Scripture. The decree was given in 458 BC but it took some time to schedule this journey and gather the necessary supplies and materials. Maybe as long as 3 to 4 years.

Notice the above three decrees are for the rebuilding of the Second Temple only.

These three decrees were not giving permission for the rebuilding of the City of Jerusalem.

Later permission was granted by King Artaxerxes to Nehemiah in approximately 445/444 BC for the rebuilding of the City of Jerusalem found in the book of Nehemiah 2: verses 1-8.

Nehemiah was allowed to travel along with some of the other Jewish captives to Jerusalem and was given materials and supplies to accomplish this rebuilding of the city.

I believe that the decree given to Ezra in the year 458 BC with the approximate date for his journey beginning in 454 BC to rebuild the Temple in Jerusalem and to Nehemiah by King Artaxerxes in 445/444 BC for the rebuilding of the City of Jerusalem marked the beginning of the 70 weeks of Daniel's End Time Vision and the ending of the 70 years of captivity as seen in a vision by the Prophet Daniel after Daniel and the other Israelite people had been in captivity for 70 years in Babylon.

Don't get confused concerning these dates, I will give you my final conclusion and summation below.

Daniel also speaks of these seventy weeks to finish Israel's transgression in the book of **Daniel Chapter 9, Verses 24 and 25** in the following scriptures.

[24] *Seventy weeks* ***(years)*** *are determined upon thy people and upon thy holy city, to finish the transgression, and to make an end of sins, and to make reconciliation for iniquity, and to bring in everlasting righteousness, and to seal up the vision and prophecy, and to anoint the most Holy* ***(talking about Jesus).***

Six things were to take place in the above Verse 24 during these 70 weeks of Daniel's End Time Vision.

1. To finish the transgression of the Jewish people. This will take place at the end of the Seven Years Tribulation Period.

2. To make an end of sins found in Romans 11: 26.

[26] *And so all Israel shall be saved: as it is written, There shall come out of Sion the Deliverer, and shall turn away ungodliness from Jacob:*

[27] *For this is my covenant unto them, when I shall take away their sins.*

3. To make reconciliation for iniquity or unrighteousness of the Jewish people as seen in the following scriptures found in Isaiah 53, Verses 3 thru 12.

[3] *He is despised and rejected of men; a man of sorrows, and acquainted with grief: and we hid as it were our faces from him; he was despised, and we esteemed him not.*

[4] *Surely he hath borne our griefs, and carried our sorrows: yet we did esteem him stricken, smitten of God, and afflicted.*

[5] *But he was wounded for our transgressions, he was bruised for our iniquities: the chastisement of our peace was upon him; and with his stripes we are healed.*

[6] *All we like sheep have gone astray; we have turned every one to his own way; and the LORD hath laid on him the iniquity of us all.*

[7] *He was oppressed, and he was afflicted, yet he opened not his mouth: he is brought as a lamb to the slaughter, and as a sheep before her shearers is dumb, so he openeth not his mouth.*

[8] *He was taken from prison and from judgment: and who shall declare his generation? for he was cut off out of the land of the living: for the transgression of my people was he stricken.*

[9] *And he made his grave with the wicked, and with the rich in his death; because he had done no violence, neither was any deceit in his mouth.*

[10] *Yet it pleased the LORD to bruise him; he hath put him to grief: when thou shalt make his soul an offering for sin, he shall see his seed, he shall prolong his days, and the pleasure of the LORD shall prosper in his hand.*

[11] *He shall see of the travail of his soul, and shall be satisfied: by his knowledge shall my righteous servant justify many; for he shall bear their iniquities.*

[12] *Therefore will I divide him a portion with the great, and he shall divide the spoil with the strong; because he hath poured out his soul unto death: and he was numbered with the transgressors; and he bare the sin of many, and made intercession for the transgressors.*

4. To bring in everlasting righteousness as found in Jeremiah Chapter 31, Verses 33 & 34.

[33] *But this shall be the covenant that I will make with the house of Israel; After those days,* ***(the seven year tribulation period and the one thousand year millennium)*** *saith the LORD, I will put my law in their inward parts, and write it in their hearts; and will be their God, and they shall be my people.*

[34] *And they shall teach no more every man his neighbour, and every man his brother, saying, Know the LORD: for they shall all know me, from the least of them unto the greatest of them, saith the LORD; for I will forgive their iniquity, and I will remember their sin no more.*

5. To seal up the vision and prophecy as found in 1 Corinthians Chapter 13, Verses 8, 9 & 10:

[8] *Charity never faileth: but whether there be prophecies, they shall fail; whether there be tongues, they shall cease; whether there be knowledge, it shall vanish away.*

[9] *For we know in part, and we prophesy in part.*

[10] *But when that which is perfect is come, then that which is in part shall be done away.* When Jesus comes back to earth to set up God's Kingdom there will not be any further need for prophesy.

6. To anoint the most Holy when Jesus returns to this Present Earth and enters the temple then the Shekinah glory will return and anoint the most Holy Place as found in Ezekiel Chapter 43, Verses 1 thru 5.

[1] *Afterward he brought me to the gate, even the gate that looketh toward the east:*

[2] *And, behold, the glory of the God of Israel came from the way of the east: and his voice was like a noise of many waters: and the earth shined with his glory.*

[3] *And it was according to the appearance of the vision which I saw, even according to the vision that I saw when I came to destroy the city: and the visions were like the vision that I saw by the river Chebar; and I fell upon my face.*

[4] *And the glory of the LORD came into the house by the way of the gate whose prospect is toward the east.*

[5] *So the spirit took me up, and brought me into the inner court; and, behold, the glory of the LORD filled the house.*

Back to Daniel Chapter 9:

[25] *Know therefore and understand, that from the going forth of the commandment to restore* ***(the Temple)*** *and to* ***(build)*** *Jerusalem unto the Messiah the Prince shall be seven weeks, and threescore and two weeks* ***(69 weeks):*** *the street shall be built again, and the wall, even in troublous times.*

These 69 weeks began at the conclusion of the seventy years that the Israeli POW's had been in exile in Babylon when Ezra was given permission to go rebuild the Temple in the time period of 458 BC and approximately four years later began his journey in 454 BC and Nehemiah was given permission to go and rebuild the City of Jerusalem in 445/444 BC and ended when Jesus made His triumphal entry into Jerusalem riding on a donkey with the people calling Him a King and His crucifixion shortly thereafter.

This was the only time I find in scripture that Jesus publicly let people acknowledge Him as being a King without rebuking them while living on our present earth and a few days later He was crucified on the cross with an inscription nailed above His head stating that **He was the King of the Jews** for everyone to see.

Let's look at the following prophetic scripture:

Zechariah 9:

[9] *Rejoice greatly, O daughter of Zion; shout, O daughter of Jerusalem: behold, thy King cometh unto thee: he is just, and having salvation; lowly, and riding upon an ass, and upon a colt the foal of an ass.*

The next time Jesus comes to Our Present Earth He will be riding on a white horse along with the Armies of Heaven made up of heavenly angels for the battle at Armageddon. Jesus will destroy the armies of the antichrist, false prophet and the northern armies of Russia (Gog-Magog) and her allies at the battle at Armageddon.

He then will set up Gods' earthly Kingdom which will last for one thousand years called the Millennium in our Bibles as seen in the following scriptures.

Revelation 19*:*

[11] *And I saw heaven opened, and behold a white horse; and he that sat upon him was called Faithful and True* ***(all His word and promises are true),*** *and in* *righteousness he doth judge* ***(all of His judgments of earth are righteous)*** *and make war.*

[12] *His eyes were as a flame of fire* ***(depicting glory and judgment),*** *and on his head were many crowns* ***(depicting total sovereignty and authority);*** *and he had a name written* ***(expresses the mystery and greatness of Jesus),*** *that no man knew, but he himself.*

[13] *And he was clothed with a vesture dipped in blood* ***(representing the judgment of Jesus' enemies):*** *and his name is called The Word of God* ***(presenting Jesus as the revelation of God Himself).***

[14] *And the armies which were in heaven followed him upon white horses, clothed in fine linen* ***(symbolizing righteousness),*** *white and clean* ***(angels, 144000 Jewish evangelist, and the tribulation saints who gave their lives for God during the tribulation period).***

[15] *And out of his mouth goeth a sharp sword* ***(depicting judgment through His spoken word),*** *that with it he should smite the nations* ***(Jesus will judge all unbelievers):*** *and he shall rule them with a rod of iron* ***(all nations will be subject to Him):*** *and he treadeth the winepress* ***(depicting His wrath)*** *of the fierceness and wrath of Almighty God.*

[16] *And he hath on his vesture and on his thigh a name written, KING OF KINGS, AND LORD OF LORDS* ***(depicts that Jesus will have universal sovereignty).***

Back to Daniel Chapter 9:

In this prophetic account God measurement was that one day stands for one year.

Sixty Nine weeks times seven days **(which one day stands for one year)** equal 483 years. The Jewish calendar uses 30 days a month multiplied by 12 months equals 360 days in a year.

Daniel 9:

[25] *Know therefore and understand, that from the going forth* ***(approximate starting time for Ezra's journey to rebuild the Temple in Jerusalem)*** *of the commandment to restore* ***(the Temple)*** *<u>and for</u>* ***(*Nehemiah*)*** *to build Jerusalem unto the Messiah the Prince* ***(triumphal entry of Jesus and His crucifixion)*** *shall be seven weeks (7), and threescore and two weeks* ***(62):*** *the street shall be built again, and the wall, even in troublous times. This totals* ***(69)*** *weeks which equals 483 years.*

In the book of Ezra Chapter 7 verses 11 thru 28 permission was granted to Ezra by King Artaxerxes for the rebuilding of the Temple in Jerusalem. This was in the year 458 BC though some time must have expired before he actually started his journey in 454 BC due to getting materials and other items ready for this journey and then permission was granted to Nehemiah in 444 BC to go and rebuild the City of Jerusalem and Jesus making His triumphal entry into Jerusalem riding on a donkey found in Matthew Chapter 21 on Palm Sunday just before his crucifixion found in Matthew Chapter 27 as the end of these 69 weeks, this will total 483 years pointed out in Daniel 9:25 above.

I submit the following calculation of the 69 weeks of Daniel's End Time Vision for the following revelations given to me in my studies.

Ezra was given permission to go to Jerusalem to rebuild the temple in the approximate year 458 BC but in the above verse 25 we do not know the actual year for the going forth **(actual date that Ezra started his journey)** as stated in this verse. If we assume that it was four years later this would be in the year of 454 BC. So if we use this year of 454 BC as our starting point this would be 454 years BC plus 30 years AD when Jesus was crucified this would equal 484 years. Sixty Nine Weeks equals 483 years so there is a one year difference which we will discuss next.

If we divide 484 years by 7 **(using the formula that 7 days equals 7 years and 7 years equals one week of this Daniels End Time prophecy)** we get a total of 69 weeks plus one year which I submit is the year between the ending of BC and the beginning of AD 1 not accounted for on the calendar. If we subtract one year between the end of BC and

AD 1 from the 484 years we get precisely 69 weeks or 483 years as stated in Daniel Chapter 9, verse 25.

The Bible just does not explain the beginning date of the 62 week time period of the Messiah being cut off in the verse below, it only give us the approximate time period for the 69 weeks.

[26] *And after threescore and two weeks shall Messiah be cut off* ***(representing the time of death of Jesus crucified on the cross)****, but not for himself* ***(Jesus did not die on the cross for Himself but He died on the cross for all mankind)****: and the people* ***(Roman Army)*** *of the prince* ***(the devil)*** *that shall come shall destroy the city and the sanctuary* ***(this was done in 70 AD by the Roman General Titus);*** *and the end thereof shall be with a flood* ***(means quickly and totally destroyed****), and unto the end of the war desolations are determined.* ***(End of the war or battle at Armageddon).***

As I previously stated above I submit to you my final conclusion and summation below.

As I studied and asked God to give me the understanding concerning these 62 weeks and 69 weeks I have reached the following conclusion. The exact beginning time is not as important as the ending time concerning these weeks and I submit the following analysis given to me concerning these 70 weeks of Daniel's End Time Vision.

I believe God in His love for all mankind inserted a break between the 69th week and the 70th week of Daniel's End Time Vision. This is the period of grace offered for the salvation to all people on our present earth who will accept Gods' Son Jesus as their savior after the Jewish people rejected Jesus as their Messiah. This includes both Gentiles and Jews. Scripture states that all things are possible with God.

I believe the time period between the 69th and 70th week represents the time period called the dispensation of Grace starting from the time of the death of Jesus on the cross until the beginning of the Seven Year Tribulation Period when this period of Grace will end.

We are currently living in this dispensation period of Grace.

Soon this period of Grace will come to an end and then comes the final 70th week described in our Bibles as the Seven Year Tribulation Period the final week of these 70 weeks of Daniels End Time Vision found in Daniel Chapter 9, verse 24.

You might ask as to why we have this time of Grace. It is because the Jewish people rejected Jesus as their Messiah and had him crucified by the Roman government and God thru His Mercy, Grace and love gave all mankind this time of Grace to either accept or deny Jesus as their Savior the Messiah.

The length of this time period of Grace is by the measurements of God not man.

God is the only one who knows when it will end and the exact time that He will come for the Church who is the Bride to present to His Son Jesus the Bridegroom.

It is only by Gods' mercy that Grace has been extended to mankind for this period of time between the 69th and 70th years of Daniel's End Time Vision.

The Seven Years of the Tribulation Period will make up the last week or the 70th week of Daniel's End Time Vision.

This final 70th week will be divided into two 3 ½ years which make up the seven years of the Seven Year Tribulation Period. This 70th week is yet to come but I believe it is coming soon.

The 70 weeks of Daniel's End Time Vision ends at the conclusion of the Seven Year Tribulation period which will also be the end of Israel's transgressions as seen in the following verse.

Daniel 9: [24] *Seventy weeks* ***(years)*** *are determined upon thy people and upon thy holy city, to finish the transgression, and to make an end of sins, and to make* *reconciliation for iniquity, and to bring in everlasting righteousness, and to seal up the vision and prophecy, and to anoint the most Holy* ***(talking about Jesus).***

Back to Daniel Chapter 9:

[27] *And he* ***(talking about the antichrist)*** *shall confirm the covenant with many* ***(talking about Israel)*** *for one week* ***(seven year tribulation period)****: and in the midst of the week* ***(after 3 ½ years)*** *he shall cause the sacrifice and the oblation to cease, and for the overspreading of abominations he shall make it desolate, even until the consummation, and that determined shall be poured upon the desolate.*

At the middle of the Seven Year Tribulation Period **(3 ½ years)** the antichrist will enter the Third Temple he approved and help to build in Jerusalem and give orders for all animal sacrifices and oblation to cease and entering into the Temple announce that he is god, thus defiling the Temple.

The people of Israel will finally recognize this man for who he is the counterfeit of the true Messiah.

This leaves 3 ½ years for the second part of the seven year tribulation period when the wrath of God will be poured out on sinful mankind living on Our Present Earth.

After these 70 weeks are over, Jesus will return to this present earth for the battle at Armageddon and then He will establish Gods' Kingdom for one thousand years known as the One Thousand Year Millennium during which time He will rule and reign over all nations on our present earth getting mankind ready for the final judgment at the Great White Thorne Judgment.

Mankind living on this earth during the One Thousand Year Millennium will be judged at the Great White Throne Judgment and the result will be to either live in Gods Kingdom on the New Earth forever throughout eternity or live with Satan and his followers for eternity in the Lake of Fire.

2Peter 3: [8] *But, beloved, be not ignorant of this one thing, that one day is with the Lord as a thousand years, and a thousand years as one day.*

This verse is not speaking in prophetic terms as we studied above in Daniel's End Time Vision but is instead talking about the measurement of time that Gods' uses.

I was mediating on this scripture found in 2Peter 3:8 above and the Holy Ghost which is our Teacher, Comforter and Guide who reminds us of things concerning Father God and Jesus brought into my understanding that in this verse concerning the measuring of time that God uses a very different formula than man uses in the measurement of time.

Mankind uses calendars, years, months, days, hours, minutes and seconds as time to rule our everyday lives on this present earth but with God there is no length in measuring time.

The revelation given to me was that one day or a thousand years with God equals all the same time. It is not the same as man's thinking in measuring time. Only man uses the terms of years, months, days, minutes and seconds to measure time as seen in the prophetic scriptures in Daniel which uses one day to equal one year.

The understanding given to me was God measures time by the magnitude of mankind's sins being committed on this present earth. Sin on our present earth will finally reach a point when God will say enough is enough and will bring an end to man's time as we know it just as He did in the days of Noah that we studied above in Part One of this book.

On our present earth today all governments have headquarters. On the New Earth the headquarters of Gods' government will be located in the Holy City New Jerusalem in the center of the Nation of Israel on the New Earth.

Many people teach and believe that we are going to live in Heaven where Gods' Throne Room is presently located for eternity but let's look at Ezekiel Chapter 45 and 48 which gives the locations and measurements for the dividing of the land in Israel for the inheritances to the twelve tribes of Israel which will be located on the New Earth.

If we were going to live in Heaven for eternity as some teach why did God give us His plan in the book of Ezekiel for the division and measurement of lands for the inheritance to the twelve tribes of Israel to live on the New Earth?

This division of land has not yet happened but will happen after the One Thousand Year Millennium when God creates the New Heaven and the New Earth.

Ladies and gentlemen this is not some man's theory or my theory this is the Word of God as written in our Bibles per the following scriptures.

Ezekiel 45:

[1] *Moreover, when ye shall divide by lot the land for inheritance, ye shall offer an oblation unto the LORD, an holy portion of the land: the length shall be the length of five and twenty thousand reeds, and the breadth shall be ten thousand. This shall be holy in all the borders thereof round about.*

[2] *Of this there shall be for the sanctuary five hundred in length, with five hundred in breadth, square round about; and fifty cubits round about for the suburbs thereof.*

[3] *And of this measure shalt thou measure the length of five and twenty thousand, and the breadth of ten thousand: and in it shall be the sanctuary and the most holy place.*

[4] *The holy portion of the land shall be for the priests the ministers of the sanctuary, which shall come near to minister unto the LORD: and it shall be a place for their houses, and an holy place for the sanctuary.*

[5] *And the five and twenty thousand of length, and the ten thousand of breadth, shall also the Levites, the ministers of the house, have for themselves, for a possession for twenty chambers.*

[6] *And ye shall appoint the possession of the city five thousand broad, and five and twenty thousand long, over against the oblation of the holy portion: it shall be for the whole house of Israel.*

[7] *And a portion shall be for the prince on the one side and on the other side of the oblation of the holy portion, and of the possession of the city, before the oblation of the holy portion, and before the possession of the city, from the west side westward, and from the east side eastward: and the length shall be over against one of the portions, from the west border unto the east border.*

[8] *In the land shall be his possession in Israel: and my princes shall no more oppress my people; and the rest of the land shall they give to the house of Israel according to their tribes.*

Ezekiel 48:

[1] *Now these are the names of the tribes. From the north end to the coast of the way of Hethlon, as one goeth to Hamath, Hazar-enan, the border of Damascus northward, to the coast of Hamath; for these are his sides east and west; a portion for Dan.*

[2] *And by the border of Dan, from the east side unto the west side, a portion for Asher.*

[3] *And by the border of Asher, from the east side even unto the west side, a portion for Naphtali.*

[4] *And by the border of Naphtali, from the east side unto the west side, a portion for Manasseh.*

[5] *And by the border of Manasseh, from the east side unto the west side, a portion for Ephraim.*

[6] *And by the border of Ephraim, from the east side even unto the west side, a portion for Reuben.*

[7] *And by the border of Reuben, from the east side unto the west side, a portion for Judah.*

[8] *And by the border of Judah, from the east side unto the west side, shall be the offering which ye shall offer of five and twenty thousand reeds in breadth, and in length as one of the other parts, from the east side unto the west side: and the sanctuary shall be in the midst of it.*

[9] *The oblation that ye shall offer unto the LORD shall be of five and twenty thousand in length, and of ten thousand in breadth.*

[10] *And for them, even for the priests, shall be this holy oblation; toward the north five and twenty thousand in length, and toward the west ten thousand in breadth, and toward the east ten thousand in breadth, and toward the south five and twenty thousand in length: and the sanctuary of the LORD shall be in the midst thereof.*

[11] *It shall be for the priests that are sanctified of the sons of Zadok; which have kept my charge, which went not astray when the children of Israel went astray, as the Levites went astray.*

[12] *And this oblation of the land that is offered shall be unto them a thing most holy by the border of the Levites.*

[13] *And over against the border of the priests the Levites shall have five and twenty thousand in length, and ten thousand in breadth: all the length shall be five and twenty thousand, and the breadth ten thousand.*

[14] *And they shall not sell of it, neither exchange, nor alienate the firstfruits of the land: for it is holy unto the LORD.*

[15] *And the five thousand, that are left in the breadth over against the five and twenty thousand, shall be a profane place for the city, for dwelling, and for suburbs: and the city shall be in the midst thereof.*

[16] *And these shall be the measures thereof; the north side four thousand and five hundred, and the south side four thousand and five hundred, and on the east side four thousand and five hundred, and the west side four thousand and five hundred.*

[17] *And the suburbs of the city shall be toward the north two hundred and fifty, and toward the south two hundred and fifty, and toward the east two hundred and fifty, and toward the west two hundred and fifty.*

[18] *And the residue in length over against the oblation of the holy portion shall be ten thousand eastward, and ten thousand westward: and it shall be over against the oblation of the holy portion; and the increase thereof shall be for food unto them that serve the city.*

[19] *And they that serve the city shall serve it out of all the tribes of Israel.*

[20] *All the oblation shall be five and twenty thousand by five and twenty thousand: ye shall offer the holy oblation foursquare, with the possession of the city.*

[21] *And the residue shall be for the prince, on the one side and on the other of the holy oblation, and of the possession of the city, over against the five and twenty thousand of the oblation toward the east border, and westward over against the five and twenty thousand toward the west border, over against the portions for the prince: and it shall be the holy oblation; and the sanctuary of the house shall be in the midst thereof.*

[22] *Moreover from the possession of the Levites, and from the possession of the city, being in the midst of that which is the prince's, between the border of Judah and the border of Benjamin, shall be for the prince.*

[23] *As for the rest of the tribes, from the east side unto the west side, Benjamin shall have a portion.*

[24] *And by the border of Benjamin, from the east side unto the west side, Simeon shall have a portion.*

[25] *And by the border of Simeon, from the east side unto the west side, Issachar a portion.*

[26] *And by the border of Issachar, from the east side unto the west side, Zebulun a portion.*

[27] *And by the border of Zebulun, from the east side unto the west side, Gad a portion.*

[28] *And by the border of Gad, at the south side southward, the border shall be even from Tamar unto the waters of strife in Kadesh, and to the river toward the great sea.*

[29] *This is the land which ye shall divide by lot unto the tribes of Israel for inheritance, and these are their portions, saith the Lord GOD.*

[30] *And these are the goings out of the city on the north side, four thousand and five hundred measures.*

[31] *And the gates of the city shall be after the names of the tribes of Israel: three gates northward; one gate of Reuben, one gate of Judah, one gate of Levi.*

[32] *And at the east side four thousand and five hundred: and three gates; and one gate of Joseph, one gate of Benjamin, one gate of Dan.*

[33] *And at the south side four thousand and five hundred measures: and three gates; one gate of Simeon, one gate of Issachar, one gate of Zebulun.*

[34] *At the west side four thousand and five hundred, with their three gates; one gate of Gad, one gate of Asher, one gate of Naphtali.*

[35] *It was round about eighteen thousand measures: and the name of the city from that day shall be, The LORD is there.*

This is exciting don't you think? God is describing in His Holy Word written many, many years ago all about the division of the land in this New Nation of Israel between the twelve tribes of Israel which will be located on the New Earth?

The Church the Bride of Christ will not live within the boundaries of this New Nation of Israel on the New Earth as some teach but will have access to the Temple of God located in this Nation of Israel. The Nation of Israel will be occupied by the twelve tribes of Israel only as seen in the above chapters and scriptures in the book of Ezekiel.

We the Church the Bride of Jesus will be ruling and reigning over many other countries and nations located on the New Earth under the direction and leadership of Jesus the Bridegroom.

Why do men and women continue to teach and preach that we will be living in Heaven for eternity when the Bible clearly states that John saw the Holy City descending down to the New Earth in Revelation 21:1?

If you ask Christians to explain what they will be doing while living in Heaven for eternity most can never explain it because they are not sure themselves, so they just make vague statements about it. No wonder it is so hard to convince sinful mankind to change their ways to accept Jesus as their Savior and to serve God.

A lot of Christians don't even know themselves what is written in the scriptures because they do not study Gods' Holy Word so how can they convince the unbeliever concerning their need to accept Jesus as their Savior.

I ran a survey on Facebook asking Christians the following question:

Do you read your bible every day and pray? The answers I got would amaze you, not good at all.

Do we as Christians have a famine for Gods' Word in our lives per the following scripture?

Amos 8: [11] *Behold, the days come, saith the Lord GOD, that I will send a famine in the land, not a famine of bread, nor a thirst for water, but of hearing the words of the Lord:*

I personally don't think we should ever leave a church service without hearing the Word of God taught.

We as Christians should be able to explain all about the New Earth that scriptures state God is going to create for us to live and reign on where there will be no more sin of any kind, just peace and joy unspeakable and full of Gods' glory.

Many Christians will not accept this teaching that we are going to live on a New Earth even though it is scriptural because their minds are so indoctrinated with past teaching concerning the Church living in Heaven in mansions for eternity.

Ladies and gentlemen we need to study Gods' Word and seek God for the true understanding and revelation of His Holy Scriptures and accept that we might have be wrong in our past teaching, preaching and beliefs and start to teach and preach the correct revelation of Gods' Holy Scriptures.

Incorrect teachings are sometimes taught because of traditions past down to us thru past teaching by others and we have just accepted it as being the truth. Sometimes these teachings are just past down from one generation to another and accepted and taught as biblical truths. Sometimes this is not intentional but just the lack of studying and praying for understanding by Christians.

I personally have heard some very strange teaching in my life time that was not biblical correct as I am sure most of you have also. If we as Christians do not study Gods' Word for ourselves, how will we know if the sermons, teaching or messages we hear or books that we read are scripturally correct?

As an example, let's look at the following scripture.

John 14: [2] *In my Father's house are many mansions: if it were not so, I would have told you. I go to prepare a place for you.*

In this verse Jesus is describing to His disciples how beautiful His Father Gods' house is with many mansions. He was not telling them or us that we have a mansion in His Father Gods' house waiting for us to live in.

How many of you have always believed and have been taught that we have a mansion prepared for us to live in when we get to Heaven? If you went to church this past week you probably heard someone talk or sing about these mansions.

I submit the following thoughts concerning the mansions mentioned in Verse Two above in John 14, Verse 2.

What would we do with a mansion since we will be spirit beings, have you ever read in Gods' Holy Word about God or Jesus living in a mansion?

Father Gods' house on the new earth will be located in the Nation of Israel occupied by the Jewish people. Only the Church will not be living in the Nation of Israel but the Church will have access to Gods' house. Since the Church will not be living in this nation, the mansions in Verse Two of John 14, Verse 2 cannot be for the Church the Bride of Christ to live in.

As spirit beings we will not need a place to eat nor will we need a place to sleep so why would we need a mansion?

We will not live as a married couple in Heaven. Reference to this is given in the below scripture, so why would we need a mansion?

Matthew 22: [30] says: *For in the resurrection they neither marry, nor are given in marriage, but are as the angels of God in heaven.*

A lot of Christians on our present earth seems to be more interested in receiving mansions than in seeing and worshiping Father God and ruling with Jesus on Gods' New Earth.

So why would we need or what would we do with a mansion? Jesus simply states that He was going to prepare a place for us.

Where do you think He is preparing us a place? I believe He is talking about preparing us a place on the New Earth which scriptures declares that we are going to rule and reign with Him.

As we will discuss below, there is no mention of nations being located in Heaven in scripture. So I ask you this question, where would we rule and reign and who would we be ruling and reigning over if we did live in Heaven for eternity? On Gods' New Earth we will rule and reign with Jesus over the earthly Gentile Nations.

I submit to you that these mansions might be for the tribulation saints who gave their lives for God during the tribulation period as seen in the following scriptures.

These saints will be servants to God in His Holy Temple located in Gods' Holy City per the following scriptures.

Revelation Chapter 7:

[13] *And one of the elders answered, saying unto me, What are these which are arrayed in white robes? and whence came they?*

[14] *And I said unto him, Sir, thou knowest. And he said to me, These are they which came out of great tribulation, and have washed their robes, and made them white in the blood of the Lamb.*

[15] *Therefore are they before the throne of God, and serve him day and night in his temple: and he that sitteth on the throne shall dwell among them.*

[16] *They shall hunger no more, neither thirst any more; neither shall the sun light on them, nor any heat.*

[17] *For the Lamb which is in the midst of the throne shall feed them, and shall lead them unto living fountains of waters: and God shall wipe away all tears from their eyes.*

In the above verse found in John 14: 2 false teaching by ministers and teachers and the lack of understanding makes people feel good about receiving and finally getting to live in a mansion in Heaven with their love ones for eternity, wading in the river of life, floating on clouds and receiving rewards in Heaven as they have been taught most all their lives even though scripture does not teach this.

This scripture does not teach that we have a mansion prepared and waiting for us in Heaven or that we will receive rewards in Heaven, it just say's that Jesus is preparing us a place.

This is just someone's personal interpretation passed down thru time that did not study or seek God for the correct interpretation and many Christians have accepted it as a biblical truth.

Scripture says that Jesus was going to prepare a place for us. It did not say that He was going to prepare us a mansion in heaven to live in. Sound's good but not scriptural.

Some ministers and teachers teach these things because they want to make their congregations feel good and keep their congregations excited about finally getting to live in a mansion which most of us do not live in on this present earth.

If they should teach something different than what their congregations have always been taught to believe, they might be call a fanatic, church attendance might decrease, the finances of the church might decrease or they might even lose their position as pastor or as a teacher for teaching and preaching something that is contrary from what people have always been taught to believe by their church denomination that they are affiliated with.

2Timothy 4: [3] *For the time will come when they will not endure sound doctrine; but after their own lusts shall they heap to themselves teachers, having* ***itching ears;***

2Timothy 2: [15] says, ***Study*** *to shew thyself approved unto God, a workman that needeth not to be ashamed, rightly dividing the word of truth.*

Many Christians when reading Gods' Holy Word read what I call surface reading and I have been guilty of this myself in the past. Ladies and gentlemen when you read Gods' word, slow down, read and comprehend what the scriptures are really saying. Ask God to give you His personal revelations' don't just accept man's interpretation.

Jesus taught a message for three years which was contrary to the teaching of the religionist leaders of His day the Scribes, Pharisees and Sadducees who had a rebellious spirit that we talked about above. They loved the praise and positions given to them by man more than God. They were more interested in what man thought about them instead of what God thought.

Do we have a rebellious spirit in our churches on our present earth today just like the Scribes, Pharisees and Sadducees did in Israel during the time of the ministry of Jesus? Are we teaching and preaching the correct Word of God or are we just going along with the teaching and preaching of the religionist leaders of our time trying to make everyone feel good?

I am not saying that all ministers and teachers have a rebellious spirit and are preaching and teaching incorrectly but many are not teaching Gods' true word.

If we do not study ourselves, how do we know the true ministers and teachers from the false ministers and teachers?

Matthew 6: [5] *And when thou prayest, thou shalt not be as the hypocrites are: for they love to pray standing in the synagogues and in the corners of the streets, that they may be seen of men. Verily I say unto you, They have their* ***reward****.*

It seems a lot of people on our present earth today have the same mindset as people did when Jesus lived and walked on our present earth. Mankind is still more interested in pleasing men instead of pleasing God, what do you think?

Sometimes we settle for good, when we could have the best.

Jesus performed miracles of healing, raising the dead, feeding multitudes and forgiving sins during His ministry on our present earth. These miracles were witnessed everyday by the religionist leader and people during the time of his ministry on our present earth and still they would not accept Him or His teaching but had Him killed. They were bogged down with traditions and rebellious spirits just like a lot of Churches and Christians are today.

Many Christians in our churches today are so closed minded, stubborn and set in their ways that they just will not accept the fact that what they have always been taught to believe could be wrong even though the scriptures proves them to be wrong.

I read a quote written in our daily newspaper by Will Rogers written on June 8, 1930 which stated that in the experiences of the everyday life of many people, that people's everyday life is just like their religion, they have their mind's made up and they don't want anybody trying to tell them what to think.

Please don't be one of these hard headed types of Christians who will not accept the truth even though the scriptures prove your previous thinking wrong. Ask and seek God to give you His true understanding and revelation of His word.

The truth is living on God's New Earth will be heavenly enjoyment for both the Church and the earthly mortal people living on the New Earth.

We the Church will be active on the New Earth ruling and reigning with Jesus over the Gentile Nations while the earthly mortal people will have an active mortal life style living on the New Earth working and raising families and worshiping God. We all will be active in praising and worshiping God and Jesus His Son for eternity.

I believe the surface of the New Earth will be just like the Garden of Eden as described in the book of Genesis, beautiful green foliage, with many different kinds of tame animals. All mankind will be in agreement with each other and we will praise and worship God for eternity.

I don't know about you but the capacity of my human brain cannot comprehend just how beautiful the New Earth is going to be, but God said that He would make all things new and that is good enough for me. Wow, Wow and another Wow!

I believe when Gods' government on the New Earth is established, just like any other government it will need workers such as presidents, governors, cabinet members, etc. that will be required to operate a government.

To me this is describing what is meant by ruling and reigning with Jesus on the New Earth that scripture says the Church as the Bride of Christ will be doing.

As previously stated I find no nations mentioned in the Bible as being located in Heaven. If there are no nations located in Heaven who and where do you think the Church Saints would be ruling and reigning with Jesus over if we are going to be living in Heaven for eternity as some teach?

If your pastor is teaching that the Church will be living in Heaven for eternity maybe you should ask him to explain to you who the Church will be ruling and reining over and explain to you where the nations will be located that the Church is going to rule and reign over with Jesus.

I submit that Gods' government with many new nations will be located on the New Earth per scripture found in Daniel 7:14 as seen below.

Daniel 7:14 states: *And there was given Him* ***(talking about Jesus)*** *dominion, and glory, and a kingdom, that all people, nations, languages, should serve Him.*

Let me explain about the New Nations on Gods' New Earth.

The New Nation of Israel will be located on the New Earth populated by those saved earthly Jewish people who lived thru the tribulation period along with the 144000 Jews made up from 12000 each of the twelve Israeli tribes and governed by the twenty four elders consisting of the twelve New Testament disciples and twelve leaders of the Old Testament.

I submit my thoughts on who these 24 elders are:

The twenty four elders will be the **(twelve)** New Testament disciples, (Simon Peter, James & John sons of Zebedee, Andrew who is the brother of Peter, Phillip, Thomas, Bartholomew, Matthew who was a tax collector, James the son of Alpheus, Simon the Canaanite, Thaddeus & Matthias.

The additional **(twelve)** will be (Moses (leader of Israel), David (a man after God's own heart), Daniel (wise man, interpreter of visions), Elijah, (Prophet) Enoch (walked with God), Abraham (father of many nations), Joseph(wise in counsel and interpreter of dreams, Joshua (leader of Israel into promise land), Gideon (leader used of God, Judge of Israel), Job (a man of endurance, example of how to trust God, Noah (dedicated obedient servant of God) & Elisha (prophet, successor to Elijah). I think the following scriptures will support my theory.

<u>Matthew 19:</u> Jesus talking to His disciples:

[28] *And Jesus said unto them* ***(talking to the twelve disciples),*** *Verily I say unto you, That ye which have followed me, in the regeneration* ***(recreation of the new earth)*** *when the Son of man shall sit in the throne of his glory, ye also shall sit upon twelve thrones, judging the* ***twelve tribes of Israel.***

<u>Luke 22:</u> [30] *That ye may eat and drink at my table in my kingdom, and sit on thrones judging the twelve tribes of Israel.* This is talking about the twelve disciples.

Where will the twelve disciples described in the above scriptures and their thrones be located? They will be located on the New Earth in the Nation of Israel per the above verses.

This pretty well explains the twenty four elders who will be ruling the twelve tribes of Israel, don't you think?

Other nations on the New Earth will be populated by those saved men and women who did not take the mark of the beast and accepted the teaching of God and lived thru the Seven Year Tribulation Period. These are not Jewish people but are people from all over the world who lived on our present earth and these nations will be ruled by the Church Saints as the Bride of Christ under the leadership of Jesus. All nations will be subject to the powers of God as seen in,

1 Corinthians 15: [28] *And when all things shall be subdued unto him, then shall the Son also himself be subject unto him (talking about God) that put all things under him, that God may be all in all.*

Just think about today's leaders and workers on our present earth, teachers, mayors, and workers in all facets of life, etc. It takes a lot of people to govern and rule a large earth.

Gods' government made up of the Church Saints will soon be implemented on the New Earth with Saints ruling in many ways in the nations on the New Earth.

For all this to be possible the world will require one super divine government with one super CEO which will be Jesus Christ.

For nearly six thousand years mankind thru the influence of Satan has tried to rule this present earth, what a mess man has made don't you agree? But read the following verse in **Daniel 7**.

Daniel 7:14 states: *And there was given Him* ***(talking about Jesus)*** *dominion, and glory, and a kingdom, that all people, nations, languages, should serve Him.*

This verse is describing Jesus as King and Ruler of Gods' Kingdom on the New Earth with people, nations, languages **(plural-different languages plus multiple nations)** serving Him. Not my words but Gods Words in Daniel 7:14 above.

When fully implemented the government of God will be a picture of harmony and unity with all those in His administration being the right choice for each job. Saints are in training on today's present earth and will be perfectly qualified for the tasks that they will face on the New Earth so be careful how you live your life on our present earth.

The Saints will be spiritual beings with heavenly bodies just like Jesus and God, having an immortal visible body not subject to gravity or other limitations of the earthly human beings.

Remember when Jesus after his death on the cross and He had risen from the tomb just walked thru the walls into the room where the disciples had gathered and they recognized Him immediately because He had a visible but spiritual body. He visited and ate with them and expounded His teaching of the scriptures and showed them the nail prints in His hands and the pierced hole in His side as found in **Luke 24: 36 thru 53**.

At another time we find Jesus walking, talking and breaking bread with two of his disciples on the road to Emmaus after His death found in **Luke 24:13**.

He also showed Himself to Mary Magdalene in **Mark 16:9**, and some other women after his death found in **Luke 24:10**.

Another time He had fish cooking on a campfire by the sea shore where Peter and some of the other disciples had gone fishing after His crucifixion. He told Peter, follow me and I will make you a fisherman of men found in **John 21:9**.

These times of visitation were before He ascended to set on His throne in Gods' throne room in Heaven where He is today.

Isaiah 9: [7] *Of the increase of his government* ***(God's government)*** *and peace there shall be no end, upon the throne of David, and upon his kingdom, to order it, and to establish it with judgment and with justice from henceforth even forever. The zeal of the LORD of hosts will perform this.*

This scripture says that there will be no end to peace on the New Earth. Think about it, what a place to live, no sin of any kind, no sickness, no deaths, just joy and peace and we get to enjoy this throughout eternity.

Isaiah 16: [5] *And in mercy shall the throne be established: and he* ***(Jesus)*** *shall sit upon it in truth in the tabernacle of David, judging, and seeking judgment, and hasting righteousness.*

Matthew 25: [31] *When the Son of man shall come in his glory, and all the holy angels with him, then shall he sit upon the throne of his glory:*

Verse 31 of Matthew 25 above states that Jesus will bring all the holy angels **(these angels will be the enforcers of the laws of God and Jesus upon all nations during the Millennium)** with Him when He returns to set up Gods' Kingdom during the One Thousand Year Millennium. It says nothing about Jesus bringing the Church with Him as some are teaching.

I believe in addition to the army of angels that Jesus will bring the 144000 Jews made up with 12000 from each of the twelve tribes of Israel who will be the evangelist to the Nation of Israel during the Millennium.

The antichrist would like to kill them but they will be sealed with Gods' seal so the antichrist cannot kill them. I believe Jesus will bring the Tribulation Saints who died and gave their lives for God during the last 3 ½ years of Tribulation Period to rule with Jesus for these one thousand years as their reward for giving their lives for God.

[32] *And before him shall be gathered all nations: and he shall separate them one from another, as a shepherd divideth his sheep from the goats:*

This is speaking about the end of the One Thousand Year Millennium and Jesus is getting the people living on our present earth ready for the Great White Throne Judgment.

The sheep are the saved Tribulation Believers both Jews and Gentiles who lived thru the Tribulation Period and those saved during the Millennium, and the goats are all the unbelievers who are alive at the end of the Millennium who did not accept Jesus as their Savior.

Also judged at the Great White Throne Judgment will be all who have died since Adam who did not accept God and Jesus as their Savior.

[33] *And he shall set the sheep on his right hand, but the goats on the left.*

[34] *Then shall the King say unto them on his right hand, Come, ye blessed of my Father, inherit the kingdom prepared for you from the foundation of the world:*

On Gods' New Earth we will enjoy some great rewards. Some rewards that came to my mind are listed below. I am sure there are many others that we will be enjoying, but I have listed six that I thought of below.

1. We will receive Eternal Life.
2. We will be ruling with Jesus on the New Earth over nations and people.
3. We will get to visit with God and Jesus in person face to face which is not possible now.
4. We will have a gloried body without any sickness, disease, or sin.
5. We will get to see our love ones, old friends and the prophets and renowned men of the Bible.
6. We will get to enjoy Gods' New Heaven and New Earth for eternity.

I do not consider myself a great bible theologian. I only write what God impresses me to write by the Holy Ghost.

A lot of people on our present earth believe they understand the truth and are right in their religionist belief because of past teachings or the teaching of their domination even though it is not what the scriptures found in Gods' Holy Word says.

Many Christians will accept what they hear or what they read on the internet as being the truth and many teach it as the truth instead of searching it out for themselves by praying and reading their Bibles thus being deceived and deceiving a lot of mankind about the truth.

I have examined myself and have had to accept that some of my past personal beliefs received thru past teaching were not scripturally correct. Sometimes this is hard to do but as I started praying, reading the scriptures with an open mind and letting the Holy Ghost reveal to me what God and Jesus wanted me to understand, not just listening to someone else's interpretation, my spiritual eyes were opened to the correct revelation of scriptures.

Ladies and gentlemen you need to read Gods' Word yourself and seek God for true understanding and revelations for yourselves.

As I begin studying the scriptures and praying for revelation and understanding, God working thru the Holy Ghost has revealed to me truths in understanding the scripture's that I misunderstood mightily in the past.

I am no different or any smarter than any of you. God does not give me special treatment or understandings that He will not give to each of you if you will only seek and ask Him.

Thousands in different religions today are being deceived by Satan and many are teaching doctrines and beliefs they believe to be true but are not. Doctrines which sometimes conflict totally with the true Word of God due to TV and internet teaching, denomination beliefs and misunderstanding of the true meaning of the scriptures.

Everywhere Jesus went while living on our present earth He spoke about the Kingdom of God which will be located on the New Earth which we will discuss below in Chapter 21 of the book of Revelation.

I realize that most Christians believe that we will be living in heaven for eternity but just read Chapter 21 of the book of Revelation and let God reveal to you the correct revelation and understanding of His Word.

The Kingdom of God was the subject of most of the parables of Jesus during His ministry on our present earth.

When Jesus commissioned His twelve apostles and sent them to preach, His instructions was to preach about the Kingdom of God, cast out devils and to heal the sick to add to the Kingdom of God as seen in the following scriptures.

Luke 9:1-2

[1] *Then he called his twelve disciples together, and gave them power and authority over all devils, and to cure diseases.*

[2] *And he sent them to preach the kingdom of God, and to heal the sick.*

Later in the following verse it says He sent out seventy other disciples, not the twelve original chosen disciples to preach about the Kingdom of God.

Luke 10: 1 *After these things the Lord appointed other seventy also, and sent them two and two before his face into every city and place, whither he himself would come.*

He also commanded them to preach about the Kingdom of God and heal the sick.

Luke 10:9 *And heal the sick that are therein, and say unto them, The kingdom of God is come nigh unto you.*

Paul preached about this same Kingdom of God's in his message everywhere he went as seen in the following scriptures.

Acts 19: 8 *And he went into the synagogue (at Ephesus), and spake boldly for the space of three months, disputing and persuading the things concerning the kingdom of God.*

Acts 20: 25 *And now, behold, I know that ye all, among whom I have gone preaching the kingdom of God, shall see my face no more.*

Acts 28: 23 *And when they had appointed him a day, there came many to him into his lodging; to whom he expounded and testified the kingdom of God, persuading them concerning Jesus, both out of the law of Moses, and out of the prophets, from morning till evening.*

Acts 28: 31_*Preaching the kingdom of God, and teaching those things which concern the Lord Jesus Christ, with all confidence, no man forbidding him.*

Jesus said the gospel was about the Kingdom of God. A lot of Christians on our present earth today just don't seem to understand or even care about what or where the Kingdom of God is. Many Christians never realize that the Kingdom of God exists or where it will be located. Many just skip this subject thinking that it is not an important subject.

Some have concluded that our local churches represent the Kingdom of God. Some believe and teach that the Kingdom of God is our saved spirit and the Kingdom of God lives within us. Some teach that the gospel of the Kingdom of God is not even for mankind today!

Ladies and gentlemen, The Kingdom of God will be a Real Earthly Kingdom that will be located on a Real New Earth as seen and described by John in Revelation Chapter 21.

If it was so important that Jesus taught and instructed his disciples to teach and preach about the Kingdom of God when He was alive and walking and teaching on our present earth, should it not be just as important for us to teach and preach that same message today?

Ladies and gentlemen examine yourself, are you preaching and teaching the truth about the Kingdom of God or are you just omitting it from your sermons and conversations.

I am not just talking about Ministers but about all Christians. It is everyone's responsibility to teach, preach and relate to others the true message concerning the future of mankind found in Gods' Holy Word while we are living on this present earth.

As we leave our journey on our present earth and began our journey in the next chapter to our New Earth, God reminded me of a scripture that Pastor Ray Mills, Pastor of Praise and Worship Church in Broken Arrow, Ok., read on Sunday morning during his message.

Matthew 7:

[13] *Enter ye in at the strait gate: for wide is the gate, and broad is the way, that leadeth to destruction, and many there be which go in thereat:*

[14] *Because strait is the gate, and narrow is the way, which leadeth unto life, and few there be that find it.*

During our journey living on this present earth whither we live or die before the Catching up of the Church we are on a journey getting us ready for the actual starting point for the beginning of our lives. This journey that we have experience on this present earth was just preparing us for the beginning of eternity in one of two places, on Gods' New Earth or in the Lake of Fire.

As we come to the conclusion of our mortal lives on this present earth, the life that we lived was getting us ready to enter in at the strait gate which leads to life eternal living on Gods' New Earth or to enter thru the wide gate that verse thirteen above says leads to destruction.

Sometimes it is easier to just follow along with the crowd traveling in the broad way but verse thirteen above says this way leads to destruction meaning those who choose this way will live for eternity in the Lake of Fire with Satan and all his followers.

CHAPTER THREE

REVELATION 21: THE NEW HEAVEN AND THE NEW EARTH

[**1**] *And I (John) saw a* ***new heaven and a new earth****: for the first heaven and the first earth were passed away; and there was no more sea.*

In this verse John makes a very profound statement saying he saw a New Heaven and a New Earth which will be created after the One Thousand year Millennium comes to a close and the judgment of mankind at The Great White Throne Judgment has been fulfilled.

The first heaven filled with lights created by God in Genesis Chapter One Verse Fourteen thru Eighteen is what we now see when we look up at the sky filled with star's, clouds, sun and the moon but this heaven will pass away and be replaced by a new heaven per the above scripture verse one.

Remember in the first part of this book we discussed God creating this first heaven in Verse Fourteen of Genesis Chapter One to block the view of His Holy City located above the earth from those inhabiting our present earth that we presently live on.

Why can't Christians accept and believe this, it is the true Word of God? Has Satan blinded the minds of Christians as to the correct message of God concerning where we are going to spend eternity?

The New Earth is where the earthly Kingdom of God will be located. Is God's Holy Word wrong when John said in the above verse one that he saw a New Heaven and a New Earth?

The New Heaven will be the firmament or atmosphere that we will see when we look up from the New Earth's surface. It will be the most beautiful blue firmament that you have ever seen, never filled with storms or tornados.

God is showing John the New Heaven and New Earth thru a vision in this Chapter Twenty One. Wow what a beautiful sight this must have been for John to see.

1Corinthians 2: [9] *But as it is written,* ***Eye hath not seen****, nor ear heard, neither have entered into the heart of man, the things which God hath prepared for them that love him.*

Why can't Ministers, Teachers and all Christians accept and teach this? This is Gods' Word written in His Holy Bible not man's word.

Have you ever wondered why during the ministry of Jesus scripture says that the Jewish people's eyes were blinded as to the true ministry of Jesus?

During the teaching by Jesus while living on our present earth He often spoke in parables. The Jewish people living on this present earth during the time of Jesus had placed all their hope in the temple and the teaching of the Law given to Moses and taught by the Jewish religionist leaders of Israel. The people just accepted the teaching of their religionist leaders instead of accepting the teachings of Jesus and putting their hope in God. Their eyes were blinded by Satan called in the bible the god of this world per the following scripture.

2Corinthians 4: [**4**] *In whom* ***the god of this world (talking about Satan the devil)*** *hath blinded the minds of them which believe not, lest the light of the glorious gospel of Christ, who is the image of God, should shine unto them.*

In the following scriptures we find this conformation. This is what they should have done.

Psalm 78:

[7] *That they might set their hope in God, and not forget the works of God, but keep his commandments:*

[8] *And might not be as their fathers, a stubborn and rebellious generation; a generation that set not their heart aright, and whose spirit was not stedfast with God.*

It seemed with every discomfort during the journey from Egypt to the promise land the children of Israel would forget God even though they saw and experienced many miracles performed by God during this journey toward the promise land after leaving Egypt.

The Jewish people during the time of Jesus had forgotten the works (miracles) of God that He had done for their forefathers after leaving Egypt and their spirit was not steadfast with God.

During the time of Jesus on earth only a few believed and accepted the teaching of Jesus even though many saw the miracles that He did everyday amongst them.

2 Corinthians 4 confirms this in verses three and four.

[3] *But if our gospel be hid, it is hid to them that are lost:*

[4] *In whom the god* ***(talking about Satan)*** *of this world hath blinded the minds of them which believe not, lest the light of the glorious gospel of Christ, who is the image of God, should shine unto them.*

I believe Jesus knew that the Jewish people were so indoctrinated with religionist traditions and beliefs and they were afraid of being banned from the temple by the religionist leaders which meant more to them than following Jesus. They were also blinded by trying to fulfill the Law given to Moses and just could not accept Jesus as their Messiah.

Jesus was teaching something new and different and the Jewish people just could not and would not accept His teaching which was contrary to the teaching of the religionist temple leaders which were trying to follow the Law given to Moses.

In **Psalm Chapter 78, Verse 11** it says: *And forgat his works, and his wonders that he had shewed them.*

We find an example of this in John Chapter 9 when Jesus healed the blind man and when the man that was healed went into the temple he was questioned by the temple religionist leaders extensively.

These temple religionist leaders would not accept that thru Jesus God had healed this man. They were more interested in keeping man's recognition than in giving God the recognition that He deserved.

*In **John 9, Verse 34** scripture says, They **(the temple religionist leaders)** answered and said unto him, Thou wast altogether born in sins, and dost thou teach us? And they cast him **(the man that was healed)** out.*

Many of our Churches today are indoctrinated with religionist traditions just like the Jewish people were during the Ministry of Jesus? Are we as Christians blinded by Satan called the god of this world?

Scripture states in ***Ephesians* 5 [27]** *That he (God) might present it to himself a glorious church, not having spot, or wrinkle, or any such thing; but that it should be holy and without blemish.*

Ladies and gentlemen God is coming for a church that is without spot, wrinkle and without blemish that will make up the Bride for His Son Jesus. **God will not accept a blemished bride for His Son.**

Are we spotless with no wrinkles or blemishes? God said that He would spew out of His mouth those that were lukewarm in the following scriptures.

Revelation 3:

[15] *I know thy works, that thou art neither cold nor hot: I would thou wert cold or hot.*

[16] *So then because thou art lukewarm, and neither cold nor hot, I will spue thee out of my mouth.*

The people of Israel had forgotten Gods' works and wonders performed during their journey from Egypt to the promise land, and we find the Israeli people during the time of Jesus had forgotten also. An example of this was when Jesus came into Jerusalem riding on a donkey and the people all shouted Hosanna to the King and laid palm branches in front of Him and a few days later these same people influenced by the temple religionist leaders were screaming crucify Him.

A lot of Christian's are doing this same thing in our churches today. God answers our prayers but soon our minds become filled with the cares of life on this present earth and we soon forget what God has done for us. Has Satan blinded our eyes?

The Jewish people believed that Jesus was a great teacher but just not their Messiah besides He came from the City of Nazareth which was contrary to the teaching of the religionist teachers of His day that nothing good could come from the City of Nazareth.

John 12:

[39] *Therefore they could not believe, because that Esaias said again,*

[40] *He hath blinded their eyes, and hardened their heart; that they should not see with their eyes, nor understand with their heart, and be converted, and I should heal them.*

[41] *These things said Esaias, when he saw his glory, and spake of him.*

[42] *Nevertheless among the chief rulers also many believed on him; but because of the Pharisees they did not confess him, lest they should be put out of the synagogue:*

[43] *For they loved the praise of men more than the praise of God.*

In the minds of the Jewish people the temple was the most holy place on this present earth and Jesus had said that He would tear down and destroy their temple and rebuild it in three days which had taken some forty six years to build as seen in the following verses.

John 2 Verses 19, 20 and 21.

[19] *Jesus answered and said unto them, Destroy this temple, and in three days I will raise it up.*

[20] *Then said the Jews, Forty and six years was this temple in building, and wilt thou rear it up in three days?*

[21] *But he spake of the temple of his body.*

Jesus was speaking about the death and resurrection of His physical body not the physical building of the temple but their carnal minds could not understand or accept this saying.

If we are not fully trusting God working thru the Holy Ghost in us, than our mortal minds can only see the carnal aspects of life not Gods' spiritual aspects for our lives just as the Jewish people were in Jesus' time.

It is the same today. Many Christian's eyes are blinded as to the true meaning of scriptures because they do not pray and study Gods' Word for themselves. Most just accept what they hear or read in some book and are content to let someone else tell them what to believe never knowing if it is scripturally correct or not.

Many Christians are afraid of being classified as being very different or fanatical if they should believe something different from what their pastor, teachers or church denomination teach just as the Jews were afraid of being banned from the temple if they accepted and believed the teaching of Jesus.

Many find it is much easier just to follow someone else than to become a true leader who will teach and preach the truth found in Gods' Holy Word.

Back to Chapter 21:

[2] *And I John saw the holy city, New Jerusalem, coming down from God out of heaven, prepared as a bride adorned for her husband.*

All the earthly people dwelling on earth will see this Holy City coming down from God out of heaven adorned with all the splendor of a Bride, WOW what a sight.

With the first heaven done away with in verse one of Revelation Chapter 21, John now has a clear view of Gods' Holy City descending down to the new created earth described in verse two.

After the One Thousand Year Millennium and the end of the Great White Throne Judgment when all sin will be removed for our present earth, God will create the New Earth and the Holy City New Jerusalem will descend to the New Earth to be located in the Nation of Israel as described in verse two above where it will take its place among many other cities on the New Earth.

There will be many other new cities located on the New Earth but the Holy City New Jerusalem will not be like any other city. It will be a very special place for in it the Temple of God and Christ will be located.

The Bride made up of Church Saints has been enjoying the beauties and wonders of Gods' Holy City since the Church was caught up and has been enjoying the Marriage Supper of the Lamb (the Lamb represents Jesus Christ) while Jesus rules for the One Thousand Year Millennium on our present earth establishing Gods' earthly kingdom. Jesus can travel between earth and Heaven in a blink of an eye so He will be present at the Marriage Supper in Heaven enjoying His Bride the Church and ruling on earth during the One Thousand Year Millennium.

I believe the Church will only be in Gods' Holy City presently located in Heaven for approximately one thousand three and one half years. This period is made up of the One Thousand Year Millennium plus the last half of the Seven Year Tribulation Period.

I believe the Bride of Christ made up of the Church Saints will descend down to the New Earth from Gods' Heaven presently located in the third heaven riding in the Holy City New Jerusalem that John is seeing in verse two above. WOW what a ride.

The Holy City New Jerusalem is presently located in Gods' Third Heaven.

You might ask just what are you talking about when you say the third heaven? Maybe you have never heard of such a place.

Please let the scriptures explain for me, Paul speaking about the third heaven.

2 Corinthians 12:

[2] *I knew a man (Paul) in Christ above fourteen years ago, (whether in the body, I cannot tell; or whether out of the body, I cannot tell: God knoweth;) such an one caught up to the* ***third heaven***. Paul was seeing this thru a vision from God.

[3] *And I knew such a man, (whether in the body, or out of the body, I cannot tell: God knoweth;)*

[4] *How that he was caught up into paradise, and heard unspeakable words, which it is not lawful for a man to utter.*

Paul a true man of God, who wrote most of the New Testament heard words and saw the beauty of Paradise, sights that his earthly mind could not even comprehend.

Just think, in the near future on the New Earth we the Church will be able to see and experience all these beautiful sights Paul was seeing and speaking about. This will be one of our rewards for eternity while living on the New Earth.

God will dwell on the New Earth in His Holy Temple in the Holy City New Jerusalem which will be located directly in the middle section of the New Nation of Israel instead of its present location in the third Heaven.

Back to Chapter 21:

[3] *And I heard a great voice out of heaven saying,* ***Behold, the tabernacle of God is with men,*** *and he will dwell with them, and they shall be his people, and God himself shall be with them, and be their God.*

Verses 1, 2 and 3 above states: *And I (John) saw a New Heaven and a New Earth, for the first heaven and the first earth were passed away and there was no more sea. And I, John saw the Holy City New Jerusalem coming down from God out of heaven prepared as a bride adorned for her husband. And I heard a great voice out of heaven saying, Behold, the tabernacle of God is with men, and He will dwell with them and they shall be His People and God Himself shall be with them and be their God.*

Praise God, this is exciting. This verse says that God will dwell with men on the New Earth not in Heaven. Ladies and gentlemen this is God's Words not my words, read verses one, two and three of this Chapter 21 again.

We the Bride will not be coming with Jesus when He comes for the battle at Armageddon and we will not rule and reign with Him when He establishes and rules over God's kingdom for the One Thousand Year Millennium. The church will still be in Heaven.

We the Bride will have already married Gods' Son Jesus in Gods' Holy City presently located in Heaven and have been enjoying the Marriage Supper of the Lamb and other beauties of Gods' Holy City.

The Bride will continue to experience the wonders and beauty of Gods' present Heaven for approximately one thousand three and one half years while Jesus the Bridegroom returns back to this present earth to set up the Kingdom of God for one thousand years which will only seem like one day.

Remember there is no measurement of time in Heaven.

Jesus seated on David's throne in Jerusalem will be ruling over the men and women living on this present earth during these one thousand years getting them ready for the final judgment at the Great White Throne Judgment.

The saved men and women who lived thru the Seven Year Tribulation Period have had children born during these one thousand years and some of these children have never made a choice between God and Satan but will have to make this choice before the end of these one thousand years.

All will be judged at the Great White Throne Judgment. The saved are the sheep and the unsaved are the goats as seen in the following scriptures.

Matthew 25:

[31] *When the Son of man shall come in his glory, and all the holy angels with him, then shall he sit upon the throne of his glory:*

[32] *And before him shall be gathered all nations: and he shall separate them one from another, as a shepherd divideth his sheep from the goats:*

[33] *And he shall set the sheep on his right hand, but the goats on the left.*

[34] *Then shall the King say unto them on his right hand, Come, ye blessed of my Father, inherit the kingdom prepared for you from the foundation of the world:*

In the following verses we find Satan being loosed out of his prison where he has been bound for one thousand years and a description of those judged at the Great White Throne Judgment.

Revelation 20:

[7] *And when the thousand years are expired, Satan shall be loosed out of his prison,*

[8] *And shall go out to deceive the nations which are in the four quarters of the earth, Gog and Magog, to gather them together to battle: the number (talking about people) of whom is as the sand of the sea.*

[9] *And they went up on the breadth of the earth, and compassed the camp of the saints about, and the beloved city: and fire came down from God out of heaven, and devoured them.*

[10] *And the devil that deceived them was cast into the lake of fire and brimstone, where the beast and the false prophet are, and shall be tormented day and night for ever and ever.*

[11] *And I saw a great white throne, and him that sat on it, from whose face the earth and the heaven fled away; and there was found no place for them.*

[12] *And I saw the dead, small and great, stand before God; and the books were opened: and another book was opened, which is the book of life: and the dead were judged out of those things which were written in the books, according to their works.*

[13] *And the sea gave up the dead which were in it; and death and hell delivered up the dead which were in them: and they were judged every man according to their works.*

[14] *And death and hell were cast into the lake of fire. This is the second death.*

[15] *And whosoever was not found written in the book of life was cast into the lake of fire.*

After the conclusions of these one thousand years and the judging at the Great White Throne Judgment is completed we the Bride will be coming back in Gods' Holy City New Jerusalem to live, rule and reign with Jesus for eternity on Gods' New Earth as recorded in this Chapter 21 of the book of Revelation.

At the conclusion of these one thousand years God will create His New Heaven and New Earth. Jesus will rule and reign along with the Church over all nations on Gods' New Created Earth except the Nation of Israel which God will rule over along with the twenty four elders that we discussed above.

If these words don't set your spirit on fire, than you better search your spiritual life and see if your pilot light has gone out and why the fire has gone out of your spirit.

In the following verse in Isaiah 65:17, John's account of the New Earth and New Heavens in Revelation 21: Verse 1 is confirmed.

Isaiah wrote these words approximately seven hundred years before John was even born.

Isaiah 65:17 says, *For, behold, I create new heavens and a new earth: and the former shall not be remembered, nor come into mind.*

Another conformation:

2 Corinthians 5: [17] *Therefore if any man be in Christ, he is a new creature: old things are passed away; behold, all things are become new.*

If we have accepted Jesus Christ as our Savior then we are a new creature so we will not remember anything about our past lives as some are teaching today.

Micah 4: 1 thru 5:

[1] *But in the last days it shall come to pass, that the mountain* ***(Temple or headquarters of Gods' Government)*** *of the house of the LORD shall be established in the top of the mountains* ***(it will be visible for miles and miles),*** *and it shall be exalted above the hills; and people shall flow unto it.*

In the following scripture verse two, nations are mentioned as being located on the New Earth in the future Kingdom of God not in Heaven:

As previously discussed I find no scriptures in our Bible that talks about nations being located in Heaven so we cannot possibly live, rule and reign for eternity in Heaven as some teach.

[2] *And many nations* ***(plural-universal)*** *shall come, and say, Come, and let us go up to the mountain* ***(means Holy Temple or headquarters of Gods' Government)*** *of the LORD, and to the house of the God of Jacob; and he will teach us of his ways, and we will walk in his paths: for the law shall go forth of Zion, and the word of the LORD from Jerusalem.*

Verses 3, 4 and 5 talks about in the Kingdom of God we will enjoy peace and universal prosperity.

[3] *And he* ***(Jesus)*** *shall judge among many people, and rebuke strong nations afar off; and they shall beat their swords into plowshares, and their spears into pruning hooks: nation shall not lift up a sword against nation, neither shall they learn war any more.* The New Earth will be filled with peace, peace and more peace.

[4] *But they shall sit every man under his vine and under his fig tree* ***(represents the place of man's residence)****; and none shall make them afraid: for the mouth of the LORD of hosts hath spoken it.*

There will not be anyone who will rob, steal, harm or make anyone afraid that lives on the New Earth as per verse four above.

[5] *For all people will walk everyone in the name of his god, and we will walk in the name of the LORD our God for ever and ever.*

Everyone will worship and walk with God for ever and ever per verse five above, what a wonderful place to live on the New Earth.

The above verses three, four and five of Micah Chapter 4, refers to the presence of God being with His people and he will forever dwell with them.

The plan of redemption has been accomplished and we will enjoy complete fellowship with God.

In this eternal state on the New Earth with God and Jesus there will be no tears, death, sorrow, crying or pain. Everything will be new.

We will not remember anything we experienced while living on this present earth as we read in **Isaiah Chapter 65 Verse Seventeen** above which says: *For, behold, I create new heavens and a new earth: and the former shall not be remembered, nor come into mind.*

Some teach that we will remember our past lives and circumstances that we encountered while living on our present earth but this is false teaching and not scriptural as seen in this verse seventeen of Isaiah Chapter 65.

Gods' promises are true and He is always faithful to His word.

Micah 4: Verses 6 and 7, speaks about the time when the Israeli people will be re-gathered back to their homeland.

[6] *In that day, saith the LORD, will I assemble her* ***(Israel)*** *that halteth, and I will gather her* ***(people of Israel)*** *that is driven out, and her* ***(people of Israel)*** *that I have afflicted;*

[7] *And I will make her* ***(people of Israel)*** *that halted a remnant, and her* ***(Nation of Israel)*** *that was cast far off a strong nation: and the LORD shall reign over them in mount Zion* ***(a ridge south of the temple in Jerusalem)*** *from henceforth, even for ever.*

This is talking about the regathering of the Israeli people from all nations on our present earth to their new homeland on the New Earth as we read above in Ezekiel Chapters 45 and 48 for the dividing of the lands for the twelve tribes of Israel.

I listened to a news report recently which reported that over one hundred thousand Jews have left the United States during the last three years. When ask why they moved back to Israel, they could not explain except the feeling in their spirit was so strong to move back to Israel that they could not resist.

Ladies and gentlemen this is scriptural and I think that we are getting very close to the beginning of the Seven Year Tribulation Period that will make up Daniel's 70th week of his End Time Vision.

Some might say that the size of the Nation of Israel as it exists today on our present earth is not big enough in size for all lands as allotted to these twelve tribes listed in Ezekiel Chapters 45 and 48.

I would have to agree with you if we were talking about the size of the Nation of Israel as it exists today on our present earth but we are talking about the size of the Nation of Israel located on the New Earth which will have plenty of room for the tribes of Israel plus Gods Holy Temple plus lands allotted for the priest who are from the tribe of the Levi to live.

There will be plenty of room on the New Earth for many other nations to be located.

Remember in Genesis 3: [8] *And they* ***(talking about Adam and Eve)*** *heard the voice of the LORD God walking in the garden in the cool of the day: and Adam and his wife Eve hid themselves from the presence of the LORD God amongst the trees of the garden.*

In the above scripture God would come down to walk and fellowship with Adam & Eve in the Garden of Eden in the cool of the day. God once again will walk and fellowship with His people on the New Earth for eternity.

What a great time we will have living on the New Earth seeing and walking hand in hand with God and Jesus.

How would you like to just take a stroll with God and Jesus holding their hands and feeling their love for you?

You will have your opportunity to do this on the New Earth if you have accepted Gods' Son Jesus as you Savior.

Back to Chapter 21:

[4] *And God shall wipe away all tears from their eyes; and there shall be no more death, neither sorrow, nor crying, neither shall there be any more pain: for the former things are passed away.*

I have heard people say that when they get to heaven they were going to ask God and Jesus to explain some things they experienced on our present earth.

This statement shows that many Christians just does not study or understand the Word of God. If they did they would have read this scripture in Revelation 21, Verse 4 which states that the former things are passed away.

We will not remember anything or even our loved ones that did not accept Jesus as their Savior. If we did we would be sad, crying and remembering all the other bad things that happened to us during our lives on this present earth.

Christians read and study Gods' word and ask God for true understanding and He will give it to you.

[5] *And he that sat upon the throne said, Behold, I make all things new. And he said unto me, Write: for these words are true and faithful.*

We will enjoy all new things. A new life filled with the wonders of the New Earth that our earthly mortal minds cannot comprehend at this time.

Gods' plan encompasses eternity. Those saints entering His Kingdom will not be idle. They will be active and productive and will continue to fulfill Gods' will and purpose.

If we prove to God that he can trust us to do His will while living on this present earth, than He will know that He can trust us to do His will on the New Earth.

If we are faithful in what He has given to us to do on this present earth then we will be rewarded with more to do living on the New Earth.

I think the following example was what Jesus was trying to explain found in the parable of the talents as seen in the following scriptures.

Matthew 25: 14-30:

[14] *For the kingdom of heaven is as a man travelling into a far country, who called his own servants, and delivered unto them his goods.*

[15] *And unto one he gave five talents, to another two, and to another one; to every man according to his several ability; and straightway took his journey.*

[16] *Then he that had received the five talents went and traded with the same, and made them other five talents.*

[17] *And likewise he that had received two, he also gained other two.*

[18] *But he that had received one went and digged in the earth, and hid his lord's money.*

[19] *After a long time the lord of those servants cometh, and reckoneth with them.*

[20] *And so he that had received five talents came and brought other five talents, saying, Lord, thou deliveredst unto me five talents: behold, I have gained beside them five talents more.*

[21] *His lord said unto him, Well done, thou good and faithful servant: thou hast been faithful over a few things, I will make thee ruler over many things: enter thou into the joy of thy lord.*

[22] *He also that had received two talents came and said, Lord, thou deliveredst unto me two talents: behold, I have gained two other talents beside them.*

[23] *His lord said unto him, Well done, good and faithful servant; thou hast been faithful over a few things, I will make thee ruler over many things: enter thou into the joy of thy lord.*

[24] *Then he which had received the one talent came and said, Lord, I knew thee that thou art an hard man, reaping where thou hast not sown, and gathering where thou hast not strawed:*

[25] *And I was afraid, and went and hid thy talent in the earth: lo, there thou hast that is thine.*

[26] *His lord answered and said unto him, Thou wicked and slothful servant, thou knewest that I reap where I sowed not, and gather where I have not strawed:*

[27] *Thou oughtest therefore to have put my money to the exchangers, and then at my coming I should have received mine own with usury.*

[28] *Take therefore the talent from him, and give it unto him which hath ten talents.*

[29] *For unto every one that hath shall be given, and he shall have abundance: but from him that hath not shall be taken away even that which he hath.*

[30] *And cast ye the unprofitable servant into outer darkness: there shall be weeping and gnashing of teeth.*

Christians we need to be able to explain to unbelievers what we will be doing while living on Gods' New Earth.

The saved earthly mortal mankind who made it thru the seven year tribulation period will have jobs, raise families and be productive on the New Earth just as mankind does and live today only without sin of any kind.

Some will be farmers, others will work in factories and other businesses just like many families are doing today only there will be peace and harmony in the work place and in their homes.

Earthly mankind will not just sit around all day enjoying the pleasures of the New Earth but will be working taking responsibility for the care of the New Earth just as Adam was instructed to do in the Garden of Eden per the following paragraph.

When God placed Adam in the Garden of Eden, he was not idle just sitting around all day, but he was working taking care of the animals and was instructed to dress and keep the Garden, meaning taking care of the Garden as seen in,

Genesis 2: [15] *And the LORD God took the man, and put him into the garden of Eden to dress it and to keep it.* Adam was instructed to work.

Mankind on the New Earth will always make time during his day to worship God. This will be the most important thing for mankind to do.

Saints will be placed in authority over all things, nations, people and the entire universe except the Nation of Israel which the twenty four elders made up of the twelve disciples from the New Testament plus the twelve Old Testament men that we discussed earlier in this book will rule over them.

What a time we are going to have while living on the New Earth!!!!

I know this may seem like very different teaching to some of you than what you have always been taught and believe but I believe it is scriptural.

During the three years that Jesus ministered to the Jewish population His teaching was different and seemed like strange teaching to the Jewish people also. He was even killed for His teaching. The religionist leaders called Him a blasphemer.

I listened to some Christian friends as they discussed an interesting subject called predestination in December 2015. Maybe you have listened or been involved in conversations about this subject yourself. I did not enter into this conversation but just listened to their discussion.

Sometimes we need to listen to other people's thoughts and maybe we can learn something or at least it will make us study Gods' word to see what it really says.

One man made a comment to me later that he had never seen me so quite when the Bible was being discussed.

I do not believe that God only predestines certain people to be saved, which I will comment on below.

Now I will give you my thoughts concerning this subject.

I believe that God in His infinite wisdom when He created mankind predestined all mankind to live for eternity and have the opportunity to become His sons and daughters born into His family. God even called Adam the son of God.

God loved His creation, both earth, man and beast.

The first spiritual test for mankind was Adam and Eve in the Garden of Eden and they failed by listening to Lucifer who was later called Satan the devil and disobeyed Gods' instructions. They could have lived for ever thru out eternity on earth if they had just followed Gods' instructions.

This changed the aspect for mankind who was predestined to live with God for eternity. After the fall of Adam and Eve, mankind is still predestined to live for eternity. Now it is either with God or Satan. It now became man's choice.

After approximately four thousand years God sent Jesus to present His plan for the redemption of mankind on our present earth.

Jesus came as a baby born in Bethlehem and when He reached the age of thirty we find Him being baptized in the river of Jordan by His cousin John and the Holy Ghost descending upon Him. This began His ministry to the Jewish people and after only three years at the age of thirty three Jesus was crucified on a cross and in doing so become the only sacrifice needed to redeem us from our sins to again become sons and daughters of God.

I believe that God in His infinite wisdom knows that all men and women will not become His sons and daughters but God thru His love for mankind gave each and every one of us a free choice in making this decision and it is ultimately our choice to accept or reject Jesus as our Savior not Gods' choice.

This is our personal choice. God had already made His choice in the beginning for everyone to receive the benefit of eternal life to live with Him.

I do not believe that God picks, chooses or predestines just certain men and women to become Christians. I believe it is God's will for all to be saved as stated in the following scriptures:

John 3:

[16] *For God so loved the world, that he gave his only begotten Son, that whosoever believeth in him should not perish, but have everlasting life.*

[17] *For God sent not his Son into the world to condemn the world; but that the world through him might be saved.*

Mankind is predestined by his own choosing to spend eternity either with God or Satan. After the fall of Adam and Eve, God gave mankind the ability to choose his own eternal destination.

Saved mankind is predestined to spend eternity with God, Jesus, the Saints and the saved Jews on the New Created Earth per the following scriptures found in Romans but only if we accept Jesus as our Savior.

Romans 8, Verses 28 thru 31:

[28] *And we know that all things work together for good to them that love God, to them who are the called according to his purpose.*

All things in this scripture is talking about Christians having the opportunity to live with God on His New Earth if we submit to His will that we are called to do on our present earth.

[29] *For whom he did foreknow, he also did predestinate to be conformed to the image of his Son, that he might be the firstborn among many brethren.*

God knows all mankind. When we accept Jesus as our Savior we take on the image of God, Jesus and the Holy Ghost thus we are predestined to live on the New Earth.

[30] *Moreover whom he did predestinate, them he also called: and whom he called, them he also justified: and whom he justified, them he also glorified.*

God predestines those who have accepted Jesus as their Savior to live on His New Earth. No unbelievers or sin will ever be present on Gods' New Earth.

God has issued a calling for us on our present earth and if we accept this calling and complete His work on this present earth we will be justified and glorified when the Church is Caught Up to become the Bride of Jesus.

[31] *What shall we then say to these things? If God be for us, who can be against us?*

With God in our lives we can live a victorious life on this present earth.

God is mindful of each of us and what we are experiencing while living on this earth and His grace is sufficient to take us thru our troubles and trials during our lifetime on this present earth as seen in the following scripture.

2Corinthians 12: [9] And he said unto me, My **grace is sufficient** for thee: for my strength is made perfect in weakness. Most gladly therefore will I rather glory in my infirmities, that the power of Christ may rest upon me.

Those who do not accept Jesus as their Savior are predestined by their own decision to live for eternity in the Lake of Fire with Satan and his followers.

So whether we live for God or Satan, we are predestined to live for eternity in one of two places, with God on His New Earth or with Satan in the Lake of Fire, it is our personal choice.

I hope my thoughts will help you in your questions about the subject of predestination.

Back to Chapter 21:

[6] *And he said unto me, It is done. I am Alpha and Omega, the beginning and the end. I will give unto him that is athirst of the fountain of the water of life freely.*

I believe we can drink from this fountain of water of life today which is referring to Gods' Spirit working thru the Holy Ghost given by God to those who are thirsty for more of His presence during our present life on this present earth.

He states that on the New Earth we can drink from His fountain of water of life freely to live for eternity. He will give it freely to us.

[7] *He that overcometh shall inherit all things; and I will be his God, and he shall be my son.*

He will not only be our God but He will be our Father and we will be His sons and daughters.

The following verses describe the Saints who will rule and reign with Jesus on the New Earth.

Matthew 5:5: *Blessed are the meek* ***(saints):*** *for they shall inherit the earth. What a promise.*

Daniel 7:27: *And the kingdom and dominion, and the greatness of the kingdom under the whole heaven, shall be given to the people of the saints of the most High* ***(God),*** *whose kingdom is an everlasting kingdom, and all dominions shall serve and obey him.*

Psalms 37:

[9] *For evildoers shall be cut off: but those that wait upon the LORD, they shall inherit the earth. No more sin on the new earth.*

Can you imagine living on the New Earth where there will never be any sin of any kind? It will truly be Joy Unspeakable and Full of Glory.

[10] *For yet a little while, and the wicked shall not be* ***(after the Great White Throne Judgment):*** *yea, thou shalt diligently consider his place, and it shall not be.*

[11] *But the meek* ***(saints)*** *shall inherit the earth; and shall delight themselves in the abundance of peace.*

[22] *For such as be blessed of him* ***(believers)*** *shall inherit the earth; and they that be cursed of him* ***(unbelievers)*** *shall be cut off* ***(sent to the lake of fire****).*

Back to Chapter 21:

[8] *But the fearful, and unbelieving, and the abominable, and murderers, and whoremongers, and sorcerers, and idolaters, and all liars, shall have their part in the lake which burneth with fire and brimstone: which is the second death.*

In this verse unbelievers will be judged at the Great White Throne Judgment and no sin of any kind will ever enter into the Kingdom of God on the New Earth.

All sin and sinners will be banished into the Lake of Fire along with Satan and his followers, this is the second death.

[9] *And there came unto me one of the seven angels which had the seven vials full of the seven last plagues, and talked with me, saying, Come hither, I will shew thee the bride, the Lamb's* ***(Jesus)*** *wife* ***(the Church the Bride of Christ).***

As previously stated the Bride of Christ will descend to the New Earth riding with our Father God in the Holy City New Jerusalem as it descends to the New Earth.

[10] *And he carried me away in the spirit to a great and high mountain, and shewed me that great city, the Holy Jerusalem, descending out of heaven from God,*

Where is the Holy City New Jerusalem descending to, out of heaven to the New Earth as seen in verse ten above?

[11] *Having the glory of God: and her light was like unto a stone most precious, even like a jasper stone, clear as crystal;*

These verses ten and eleven are describing the Holy City New Jerusalem and the Shekinah Glory of God shinning on the New Earth.

The following verses twelve thru seventeen describes the size of the Holy City New Jerusalem as being fifteen hundred miles in length, breath, height, all equal and a wall two hundred sixteen feet high surrounding it per the measurement of man.

What a sight. This Holy City will be a breath taking sight which we will get to see.

Sometimes we see the White House, Lincoln Monument or other Government Buildings in Washington DC and think what beautiful buildings and a beautiful capitol city we have in the United States.

The Holy City New Jerusalem with Gods Temple located in it will be so beautiful that it will make all building and cities on our present earth look like slum areas compared to the beauty of it.

Praise the Lord, I am getting excited just writing and thinking about what we are going to enjoy and experience while living on the New Earth.

I hope as you are reading this book that you are getting excited about the New Earth and the role you will be involved in while ruling and reigning with Jesus.

[12] *And had a wall great and high (shows the enormous size of the Holy City surrounded by this great wall), and had twelve gates, and at the gates twelve angels, and names written thereon, which are the names of the twelve tribes of the children of Israel:*

[13] *On the east three gates; on the north three gates; on the south three gates; and on the west three gates.*

These gates show complete accessibility to the Holy City, no gates ever closed.

[14] *And the wall of the city had twelve foundations, and in them the names of the twelve apostles of the Lamb.*

One foundation named after each of the twelve apostles. What a place to have your name inscribed, maybe on a golden or bronze plaque.

[15] *And he that talked with me had a golden reed to measure the city, and the gates thereof, and the wall thereof.*

Even the instrument of measurement is made of gold. Ladies and gentlemen how would you like to have a golden tape measure, I sure would?

[16] *And the city lieth foursquare, and the length is as large as the breadth: and he measured the city with the reed, twelve thousand furlongs.*

The length and the breadth and the height of it are equal. Fifteen hundred miles high, equal on every side by the measurements of man.

[17] *And he measured the wall thereof, an hundred and forty and four cubits, according to the measure of a man, that is, of the angel.*

This is approximately two hundred sixteen feet high per the measurements of man.

The following verses eighteen thru twenty one depicts earthly materials that we are acquainted with on our present earth now described as glorified materials on the New Earth. They depict the glory, beauty and eternal quality of the Holy City New Jerusalem.

[18] *And the building of the wall of it was of jasper: and the city was pure gold, like unto clear glass.*

There has never been a city on this present earth as beautiful as this city will be, and just think if we have accepted Jesus as our Savior we will get to enjoy it for eternity.

[19] *And the foundations of the wall of the city were garnished with all manner of precious stones.*

The first foundation was **JASPER (comes in a variety all colors, mostly striped, spotted or flamed usually red, yellow, brown or green)**; the second, **SAPPHIRE (blue);** the third, a **CHALCEDONY**, **(colors are bluish, white, or gray);** the fourth, an **EMERALD (green);**

[20] *The fifth,* ***SARDONYX (red with alternating brown and white bands);*** *the sixth,* ***SARDIUS (blood red, the first stone in the High Priest breastplate);*** *the seventh,* ***CHRYSOLITE (yellow and gold);*** *the eighth,* ***BERYL (green, red, gold with clear crystal)****; the ninth, a* ***TOPAZ (comes in many colors, including clear, brown, yellow, orange, red, pink and blue)****; the tenth, a* ***CHRYSOPRASUS (golden/green);*** *the eleventh, a* ***JACINTH (reddish blue or deep purple)****; the twelfth, an* ***AMETHYST (brilliant purple).***

Can you imagine the beauty of these precious stones sparkling from the Shekinah Glory of God? Can you imagine what a sight this is going to be?

[21] *And the twelve gates were twelve pearls; every several gate was of one pearl: and the street of the city* ***(only one street)*** *was pure gold, as it were transparent glass.* Gold that is so pure that it looked like glass.

Wow, what a sight to behold, the effects is a magnificent city of brilliant transparent gold adorned with gems of every color with the street of this city made of pure radiant gold looking like transparent glass the color of pure gold.

WOW, WOW, WOW WHAT A SIGHT.

As I am writing this book my Spirit can hardly wait, is says in:

Revelation 22: [20] ***He which testifieth these things saith, Surely I come quickly. Amen. Even so, come, Lord Jesus.***

My Spirit also says come quickly Father God for the Catching up of your children the Church so that we can marry Your Son Jesus and then He can return to this present earth to set your Kingdom. In the Old Testament Gods' instruction for the tribes of Israel was to marry within their own blood line. You and I if we have accepted Jesus as our Savior have the same blood line as God and Jesus. So when we marry Jesus we will be in perfect harmony with Gods' laws given to Moses.

The Bride the Church will be ready to come back to the New Earth to rule and reign with Jesus for eternity. This will happen after the One Thousand Year Millennium.

[22] *And I saw no temple therein: for the Lord God Almighty and the Lamb are the temple of it.*

[23] *And the city had no need of the sun, neither of the moon, to shine in it: for the glory of God did lighten it, and the Lamb is the light thereof.*

This represents the Shekinah Glory which is the Divine Glory of God and will light up the whole city. What a sight! I can hardly wait to see this city, what about you?

[24] *And the nations of them which are saved shall walk in the light of it: and the kings of the earth do bring their glory and honour into it.*

Again speaking of the nation's which will be located on the New Earth and their leaders bringing glory and honour into it.

[25] *And the gates of it shall not be shut at all by day: for there shall be no night there.*

This shows that no security is needed. We will have complete accessibility to Gods' Holy City and His Throne Room. Daylight is continuous since darkness never comes.

[26] *And they shall bring the glory and honour of the nations into it.*

The people and nations will be holy, no sin, a perfect earth to live on.

[27] *And there shall in no wise enter into it anything that defileth, neither whatsoever worketh abomination, or maketh a lie: but they which are written in the Lamb's book of life.*

Only the redeemed people of God will have access to the Throne Room and Temple in the New Holy City New Jerusalem on the New Earth.

No sin will ever be able to enter or be on the New Earth after it is created by God. What a place to live. Are you getting excited, I am?

After the One Thousand Year Millennium is over, God will create a New Heaven and a New Earth and dwell with mankind on the New Earth in His Holy Temple located in the Holy City New Jerusalem located directly in the middle of the New Nation of Israel instead of its present location in the third heaven.

John records the time when he saw the Holy City New Jerusalem descending down to earth from Heaven in:

Verse Two of Chapter 21: *And I John saw the holy city, New Jerusalem, coming down from God out of heaven, prepared as a bride adorned for her husband.*

Revelation 21 pictures the last phase of Gods' Master Plan for mankind with the establishment of the New Heaven, the New Earth and the New Holy City New Jerusalem located on the New Earth.

Jeremiah 33: 16 says that Jerusalem shall be called THE LORD OUR RIGHTEOUSNESS. WOW

Ezekiel 48:35 says that Jerusalem shall be called THE LORD IS THERE. WOW!

2Peter 3: 10 thru 13 say's:

[10] *But the day of the Lord will come as a thief in the night; in the which the heavens shall pass away with a great noise, and the elements shall melt with fervent heat, the earth also and the works that are therein shall be burned up.*

The works in the above scripture depicts man's establishments and all traces of the sins of man located on this present earth which will be burned up.

[11] *Seeing then that all these things shall be dissolved, what manner of persons ought ye to be in all holy conversation and godliness,*

[12] *Looking for and hasting unto the coming of the day of God, wherein the heavens being on fire shall be dissolved, and the elements shall melt with fervent heat?*

[13] *Nevertheless we, according to his promise, look for new heavens and a new earth, wherein dwelleth righteousness.*

I have given you scriptures in this book to support the teaching about God creating a New Earth. Saved mankind will be living on the New Earth for eternity not in Heaven as many teach. I hope by now you believe that we will live on the New Earth with God, Jesus and all our saved brothers and sisters for eternity?

After the One Thousand Year Millennium the headquarters of Gods' Government will be located on the New Earth in the center of the Nation of Israel.

At that time Jesus will turn over the Kingdom to Father God.

God the Son Jesus will sit on the Throne of David in Jerusalem and rule all nations along with His Bride made up of Church Saints.

This government will continue to grow, without end, and the Temple of God will be here on the New Earth. Read Chapter 21 again to see the beauty of it.

You might ask, how can the government or population continue to grow for eternity on the New Earth? Please let me explain.

The saved Tribulation Saints from all over the world on our present earth and the remnant of Jews saved in Israel who live thru the tribulation period both will still be able to marry and conceive children and will replenish the New Earth for eternity thus the population on the New Earth will continue to grow.

These are saved earthly men and women with earthly mortal bodies. They will live and have earthly duties such as working, raising families but they will get to enjoy the presence of God just like the Church except they will have mortal bodies without sin.

But those who gave their lives during the last three and one half years of the tribulation period called the Great Tribulation Saints and the Church Saints that was saved during the period of grace will have a spiritual glorified visible body just like God, Jesus and the angels, thus not able to reproduce.

The Tribulation Saints will be servants in Gods' Temple which we will discuss in Chapter Twenty Two below and the Church Saints will be kings and priest and will rule and reign with Jesus over all nations on earth with the exception of the Nation of Israel.

CHAPTER FOUR

REVELATION CHAPTER 22: DESCRIBES GOD'S TEMPLE LOCATED ON THE NEW EARTH

[1] *And he shewed me a pure river of water of life, clear as crystal, proceeding out of the throne of God and of the Lamb.*

Notice the similarity of the following scriptures found in **Ezekiel Chapter 47 below and Verse One of Revelation 22 above.** They are speaking about the same pure river of the water of life flowing out of the throne of God and of the Lamb.

This river will flow out from the throne of God making its way down into the Dead Sea and will bring this sea alive with all manner of sea creatures living in it:

Nothing can live in this sea now because of the salt content but these waters will be healed as seen in the following scriptures.

Ezekiel 47:

[8] *Then said he unto me, These waters issue out toward the east country, and go down into the desert, and go into the sea: which being brought forth into the sea, the waters shall be healed.*

This is speaking about the healing of the waters of the Dead Sea. This will not be called the Dead Sea anymore after this for this sea will come alive.

This is the same for mankind, when God takes our dead spirit and renews it and it is healed and brought back alive by accepting Jesus as our Savior, then we become a living soul just like when God created man in the beginning when He breathed His breath of life into man and scripture states that man became a living soul. This body of water will be a living sea.

This is exciting, I say come quickly Lord Jesus.

[9] *And it shall come to pass, that everything that liveth, which moveth, whithersoever the rivers shall come, shall live: and there shall be a very great multitude of fish, because these waters shall come thither: for they shall be healed; and everything shall live whither the river cometh.*

[10] *And it shall come to pass, that the fishers shall stand upon it from En-gedi (located on the western shore of the dead sea) even unto En-eglaim (mentioned only one time in the bible-a place on the Dead Sea); they shall be a place to spread forth nets; their fish shall be according to their kinds, as the fish of the great sea, exceeding many.*

This verse ten of Ezekiel Chapter 47 should be exciting for you men and women who love to fish. How would you like to go fishing in the healed waters of the Dead Sea that was brought back to life? No one has ever caught a fish from this sea but this will be possible once these waters are healed and it becomes alive with all manner of sea creatures living in it.

This could be one of your rewards if you accept Jesus as your Savior and live on Gods' New Earth.

[11] *But the miry places thereof and the marshes thereof shall not be healed; they shall be given to salt.*

Have you ever wondered why the miry places and marshes were not healed? I have and below I give to you some of the result of my studies.

Salt marshes are coastal wetlands that are flooded and drained by salt water brought in by the tides. They are marshy because the soil is composed of deep mud, decayed wood and plant matter sometimes called peat.

These habitats are essential for food and refuge for many sea species including shrimp, crab and many finfish that require salty waters to live so these salt marshes will stay salty for the sea creatures created by God that needs salt waters to survive after He heals the waters of the Dead Sea.

Salt marshes also protect shorelines from erosion by trapping sediments.

This is some of man's explanation for marshes but I believe God already knew this so this is why the marshes located by the present Dead Sea per verse eleven above will not be healed but will stay salty after the water of this sea is healed and brought alive.

God thinks of everything, don't you agree?

[12] *And by the river upon the bank thereof, on this side and on that side, shall grow all trees for meat, whose leaf shall not fade, neither shall the fruit thereof be consumed: it shall bring forth new fruit according to his months, because their waters they issued out of the sanctuary: and the fruit thereof shall be for meat, and the leaf thereof for medicine.*

In the above verse twelve of Ezekiel these trees will have an abundance of fruit for us to eat and the leaves are for medicine. The medicine from these leaves are for the healing of the nations or people who live in them to receive eternal life as seen in verse two below.

Twelve different kind of fruit every month and will never run out.

What a place, I can't even imagine what it will be like, can you?

Back to Chapter 22:

[2] *In the midst of the street of it, and on either side of the river* ***(this is the river flowing from Gods Throne down into the Dead Sea)****, was there the tree of* *life, which bare twelve manners of fruits, and yielded her fruit every month: and the leaves of the tree were for the healing of the nations.*

This description is very similar to verse twelve in Ezekiel Chapter 47 we just read above.

The above scripture describes two fruit bearing trees of life, one on either side of the river. I believe one is for earthly mortal people of the Nation of Israel and one is for the earthly mortal people of the Gentile Nations for their healing to receive eternal life. The Church, the Bride of Christ already has received eternal life.

The healing here is speaking of living and receiving eternal life without the curse of sin placed on mankind thru the disobedience to God by Adam and Eve in the Garden of Eden.

These trees picture eternal substance and morality. The leaves are for the healing of all people both Jewish and Gentile, giving them eternal life.

[3] *And there shall be no more curse: but the throne of God and of the Lamb shall be in it; and his servants shall serve him:*

The curse in this verse is talking about the removal of the sin curse placed on man after the fall of Adam and Eve when they were removed from the Garden of Eden.

The servants in this verse are the tribulation saints who gave their lives during the tribulation. They will be Gods' temple servants as seen in the following scriptures.

Remember we discussed above that the mansions located in Gods' Holy City might be for these tribulation saints who gave their lives for God during the last 3 1/2 years of the tribulation period.

Revelation 7:

[13] *And one of the elders answered, saying unto me, What are these which are arrayed in white robes? and whence came they?*

[14] *And I said unto him, Sir, thou knowest. And he said to me, These are they which came out of great tribulation, and have washed their robes, and made them white in the blood of the Lamb.*

[15] *Therefore are they before the throne of God, and serve him day and night in his temple: and he that sitteth on the throne shall dwell among them.*

[16] *They shall hunger no more, neither thirst any more; neither shall the sun light on them, nor any heat.*

[17] *For the Lamb which is in the midst of the throne shall feed them, and shall lead them unto living fountains of waters: and God shall wipe away all tears from their eyes.*

Back to Chapter 22:

[4] *And they shall see his face; and his name shall be in their foreheads.*

Satan knows the scriptures and he is a counterfeiter who causes mankind to receive his mark during the end times and always tries to imitate God as seen in Revelation 13 [16] *And he causeth all, both small and great, rich and poor, free and bond, to receive a mark in their right hand, or in their foreheads:*

Seeing Gods' face will be one of the greatest blessings and rewards for mankind for eternity. We will be able to look into the faces of God and Jesus.

This is now impossible for an un-glorified mortal human being but it will be possible in the eternal state with God when we receive our heavenly glorified bodies.

The name of God in our foreheads signifies ownership and consecration.

[5] *And there shall be no night there; and they need no candle, neither light of the sun; for the Lord God giveth them light: and they shall reign for ever and ever.*

Since God is always present in the Holy City New Jerusalem His Divine Shekinah Glory makes all other sources of light unnecessary. Gods' presents will lighten the whole city.

[6] *And he said unto me, These sayings are faithful and true: and the Lord God of the holy prophets sent his angel to shew unto his servants the things which must shortly be done.*

[7] *Behold, I* ***(God)*** *come quickly: blessed is he that keepeth the sayings of the prophecy of this book.*

[8] *And I John saw these things, and heard them. And when I had heard and seen, I fell down to worship before the feet of the angel which shewed me these things.*

In this verse John certifies that he saw and heard these things and has written them down in the Book of Revelation in our Bible for our benefit.

[9] *Then saith he* ***(the angel who showed John these things)*** *unto me, See thou do it not: for I am thy fellow servant, and of thy brethren the prophets, and of them which keep the sayings of this book: worship God.*

John shows the human side of himself by falling down at the feet of the angel to worship the angel. The angel rebukes him for this because angels are simply servants of God and not to be worshiped.

[10] *And he saith unto me, Seal not the sayings of the prophecy of this book: for the time is at hand.*

In contrast to John, Daniel was told to seal up the prophecies of his book until the time of the end found in Daniel 12:4 while John was told to leave his book open **(says seal not)** in Revelation 22:10 which states that the time of the end is at hand.

The time at hand or the time of the end represents the Messiah Jesus the Son of God coming and establishing the Kingdom of God which will last for eternity.

[11] *He that is unjust, let him be unjust still: and he which is filthy, let him be filthy still: and he that is righteous, let him be righteous still: and he that is holy, let him be holy still.*

This verse is not a command but a statement of fact and warnings concerning the spiritual condition of mankind judged at the final White Throne Judgment.

[12] *And, behold, I come quickly; and my reward is with me, to give every man according as his work shall be.*

Verse 12 says *Behold, I* ***(Jesus Christ)*** *come quickly, and my reward* ***(Saints position in God's government on the New Earth)*** *is with me, to give every man according as his work* ***(man's experience of work done on our present earth)*** *shall be.*

Jesus Christ the Son of God is coming down to this present earth at the beginning of the One Thousand Year Millennium to establish His Father Gods' Kingdom.

He will give rewards to the Saints when they along with the Holy City New Jerusalem return to the New Earth at the conclusion of the One Thousand Year Millennium.

Some teach that the Church made up of Saints are going to Heaven to receive rewards but look again at verse twelve above to see the correct statement of Jesus.

The saints are not going to live in Heaven for eternity but will live here on the New Earth in the earthly Kingdom of God for eternity.

After the One Thousand Year Millennium the deliberate choice of each and every person living on our present earth will have fixed his or hers eternal fate for eternity.

If your name is written in the Book of Life you will receive eternal life and given the opportunity to live on the New Earth for eternity but if your name is not found written in the Book of Life you will also receive eternal life destined to live in the Lake of Fire with Satan and his followers for eternity.

[13] *I am Alpha and Omega, the beginning and the end, the first and the last.*

God was here in the beginning and verse thirteen above says He will be here at the end of this present earth and He will be here on the New Earth for eternity with all those who have accepted His Son Jesus as their Savior for ever and ever.

Have you done this today, if not, please accept Jesus as your Savior today and live with me for eternity on God's New Earth.

[14] *Blessed are they that do his commandments, that they may have right to the tree of life, and may enter in through the gates into the city.*

Gods' promise to mankind in verse fourteen above depicts Heavenly Citizenship in the dwelling place of Gods' Kingdom which covers the whole New Earth and accessibility to The Holy City New Jerusalem of God located on the New Earth.

[15] *For without are dogs* ***(impure people),*** *and sorcerers* ***(those who practice witchcraft),*** *and whoremongers* ***(those who practice sexual immorality),*** *and murderers* ***(someone who takes the life others),*** *and idolaters* ***(those who worship idols or other gods),*** *and whosoever loveth and maketh a lie.*

Verse 15 is describing those who were unwilling to repent of their degenerate lifestyles while living on our present earth will never live in the Kingdom of God on the New Earth but will spend eternity in the Lake of Fire along with Satan, demons, fallen angels, antichrist, false prophet and all other unbelievers.

These things God hates see **Proverbs 6:16 thru 19** which describes seven deadly sins.

[16] *These six things doth the LORD hate: yea, seven are an abomination unto him:*

[17] *A proud look, a lying tongue, and hands that shed innocent blood,*

[18] *A heart that deviseth wicked imaginations, feet that be swift in running to mischief,*

[19] *A false witness that speaketh lies, and (seventh) he that soweth discord among brethren.*

We should be very careful to follow Gods' commandments and not commit sins as stated in the above verses otherwise we will not have a right to the tree of life and not have access to Gods' Holy City on the New Earth.

We need to search our lives daily and if we have any of the above sins in our lives we need to get rid of them as soon as possible.

Sometimes we get so complacent while serving God that we get caught up in the cares of life while living on our present earth and we think nothing about these sins as being deadly sins in our everyday life. This is a device of Satan to blind our eyes and mind to the will of God for our lives.

Back to Chapter 22:

[16] *I Jesus have sent mine angel to testify unto you these things in the churches. I am the root and the offspring of David, and the bright and morning star.*

This verse sixteen is describing Jesus as a descendant of King David. He's the bright and morning star and in this verse He indicates that this revelation is for everyone.

[17] *And the Spirit and the bride say, Come. And let him that heareth say, Come. And let him that is athirst come. And whosoever will, let him take the water of life freely.*

The Spirit in this verse in in reference to the Holy Ghost and the Bride speaking is none other than the Church.

The Holy Ghost and the Church are issuing an invitation **three times** in verse seventeen for the un-saved to come to Christ and accept Him in faith to receive eternal life to live on Gods' New Created Earth.

[18] *For I testify unto every man that heareth the words of the prophecy of this book, If any man shall add unto these things, God shall add unto him the plagues that are written in this book:*

This is a warning from Jesus given thru John warning mankind to not add unto these things.

Sometimes men give their own personal interpretation of Gods' Word and teach their interpretations as biblical truths. This verse states that God will send plagues upon men who add and teach their own interpretations of Gods' Word as truths which deceive mankind when they are not biblical truths.

We should seek God and ask Him for the true understanding of His word as seen in the following scripture.

Matthew 7: [7] *Ask, and it shall be given you;* ***seek****, and ye shall find; knock, and it shall be opened unto you:*

We should not add or take away from His word as stated in verse nineteen below.

[19] *And if any man shall take away from the words of the book of this prophecy, God shall take away his part out of the book of life, and out of the holy city, and from the things which are written in this book.*

Verses 18-19 is a warning by God aimed against the willful distortion of the message of this book. This could mean man's personal interpretation of these scriptures and teaching them as biblical truths or false teaching of scriptures just because of what we have always been taught and not willing to change our thoughts and beliefs.

[20] *He which testifieth these things saith, Surely I come quickly. Amen. Even so, come, Lord Jesus.*

John is testifying to these things in this verse and is saying come quickly Lord Jesus in this verse. I also say come quickly Lord Jesus. Do you feel this way, I sure hope so?

This is the final promise of God in the Bible that His return is imminent and for the return of Jesus to set up Gods' Kingdom on our present earth during the One Thousand Year Millennium. Amen means SO BE IT.

Becoming a Christian means a total change and a total different way of life. If you have accepted and belong to Christ then your eyes and thoughts should be fixed on the Kingdom of God and striving to become a citizen of Gods' Kingdom.

It should be the greatest goal in life for mankind to become a citizen in the Kingdom of God when Jesus sets up Gods' Government on the New Earth. This is done by accepting Jesus as your Lord and Savior.

God has purposed that those who make up the Church who is the Bride of Christ become part of His God Family. The Bride will not be of physical earthly flesh but of spiritual heavenly flesh with eternal life in the Kingdom of God on the New Earth.

There will be earthly men and women living on the New Earth in Gods' Earthly Kingdom and will make up Gods' earthly family but they will not be part of Gods' Spiritual Family. These earthly men and women are the ones who accepted God and lived thru the tribulation period or were born during the Millennium that accepted Jesus as their Savior.

Only those who have accepted Jesus as their Savior during our present time of grace on our present earth and those who gave their lives during the tribulation period and the saints of old will be born into Gods' Spiritual Family.

Jesus Christ was the first to be crowned with glory and honor in the God Family. It is through Jesus Christ that many sons and daughters will be brought into that same glory, born into the God Family actually begotten as sons and daughters (yet unborn) of God until the Catching up of the Church.

Remember that the Church is the Spiritual Bride of Christ and the Jewish people of the Twelve Tribes of Israel who lived thru the tribulation period are Gods' chosen earthly people who make up the New Nation of Israel on the New Earth.

Israel will be an earthly nation located in Gods' earthly Kingdom with the Holy City New Jerusalem and the Temple of God located directly in the middle of the New Nation of Israel.

There will be many other earthly gentile people, cities and nations located on the New Earth made up of those earthly people who lived thru the tribulation period who accepted God.

What a wonderful New Earth it is going to be for us to live on, a true Garden of Eden.

We can overcome sin through prayer, studying Gods' Holy Word and receiving the revelation of Gods' Word, living by faith and thru our daily experiences of life in Christ we can overcome sin as seen in the below verse.

Ephesians 3: [20] *Now unto him* ***(God)*** *that is able to do exceeding abundantly above all that we ask or think, according to the power* ***(Holy Ghost)*** *that worketh in us,*

Thru trials and testing's we will grow spiritually more and more like God until at the time of the New Created Earth we the Bride of Christ will return in the Holy City that John saw descending down from heaven to the New Earth to rule and reign with Jesus for eternity.

At the Catching up of the Church we shall than be born of God actually born into the God Family as Sons and Daughters of God and become the Bride for His Son Jesus!

Think about it, those that make up the Bride will actually be Sons and Daughters of God born into the God Family and Jesus will be our Bridegroom.

Jesus will be King of Kings and Lord of Lords over all the New Earth.

WOW, WOW, and WOW!

Do you really believe this? As we grasp this tremendous, wonderful truth, our minds will be filled with joy unspeakable and full of glory.

Thank you for letting me share with you my thoughts and revelations in the writings of this book given to me by God thru the Holy Ghost during my studies of Gods' Holy Word.

I hope you were blessed as you read this book concerning Our Present Earth and the New Earth to Come.

I have prayed and ask God for wisdom and to give me true understanding of His Holy Scriptures concerning the New Earth.

We started our journey in the first part of this book with God creating a man by the name of Adam and placing him in the Garden of Eden located on our present earth. This present earth has experience some drastic changes due to sin since God created this man.

This present earth that we live on is the same earth that God created in the beginning found in Genesis Chapter One Verse One below. Jesus walked, lived and died on this same earth that we live on today.

At the conclusion of this book we read about a New Earth that God will once again create just as beautiful as it was when God created the first earth as stated in **Genesis Chapter One, Verse One** which says: *In the beginning God created the heaven and the earth.*

This New Earth will never experience any sin on it and it will last for eternity. It will truly be a place of Joy Unspeakable and Full of the Glory of God.

If you are not a believer I hope something that I have written and shared with you in this book will encourage you to become a Christian and to live with me in the Kingdom of God forever on this New Earth along with all my brothers and sisters in Christ.

Ecclesiastes: 12:13 says, *Let us hear the conclusion of the whole matter, Fear God, and keep His commandments, for this is the whole duty of Man.*

I have and will always try to back up my thought and writings with the Holy Scriptures, not just my theory, but by Gods' word.

Harley Denny

ABOUT THE AUTHOR

God was the spiritual author, i was only the earthly co-author given His revelation concerning man's future for my readers of this book. The book, The Final Destination of Man was also written by this author.

#0188 - 030217 - C0 - 229/152/16 - PB - DID1744845